PRAY BALL!

PRAY BALL!

The Spiritual Insights of a Jewish Sports Fan

Rabbi James Gordon

gefen
publishing house בית ההוצאה לאור

JERUSALEM ◆ NEW YORK

Typesetting: Marzel A.S. — Jerusalem
Cover Design: Studio Paz, Jerusalem

Edition 9 8 7 6 5 4 3 2

Gefen Publishing House
POB 36004
Jerusalem 91360, Israel
972-2-538-0247
isragefen@netmedia.net.il

Gefen Books
12 New Street
Hewlett, NY 11557, USA
516-295-2805
gefenbooks@compuserve.com

www.israelbooks.com

Printed in Israel   *Send for our free catalogue*

Library of Congress Cataloging-in-Publication Data
Gordon, James M., 1958-
Pray Ball: The Spiritual Insights of a Jewish Sports Fan / James M. Gordon
    p.   cm.
Includes bibliographical references.
ISBN: 965 229 219 2

1. Sports—Relgious aspects—Judaism. 2. Sports—United States Anecdotes. 3. Ethics, Jewish. 4. Sports—
Moral and ethical aspects—United States.   I. Title.
GV706.42.G67   1999
296.7'2—dc21
                                                     99-36607
                                                       CIP

*This book is dedicated with love
to the most important "team" in my life — my family:
my parents Rabbi Nathan and Esther Gordon,
and my wife Marilyn and our children Max, Rita and Sophia.*

Contents

BASEBALL: A Season for Being Born

BASKETBALL: A Season for Dancing

FOOTBALL: A Season for Breaking and Building

ACKNOWLEDGEMENTS

Hakarat ha-tov. In the world of sports it is expressed by "high fives," hats thrown onto the hockey rink, standing ovations, trophies and performance bonuses. In Jewish tradition, it is manifested by handshakes, honoree dinners and by simply saying, "thank you."

Hakarat ha-tov means "recognizing the good." It refers to recognizing a job well done, by giving credit where credit is due.

Pray Ball! The Spiritual Insights of a Jewish Sports Fan has come to fruition through the support and assistance of many people. In the spirit of *hakarat ha-tov,* it is important particularly to recognize and thank some of these individuals.

- My parents, Rabbi Nathan and Esther Gordon, for bringing me into this world and for instilling in me the importance of combining and applying Jewish and secular education to help make our world a better place.

- My wife Marilyn for her love, support and honest critiques of my work.

- Our children Max, Rita and Sophia for graciously allowing me to use some of our precious Jewish Quality Time together to complete this project.

- My "Aunt" Rae (of blessed memory) and "Uncle" Lenny Hochman for inspiring me to become a sports fan by taking me to my first sporting event — a Chicago White Sox game.

- Lou Weisbach for his support, friendship and patience.

- Leigh Steinberg who, along with Lou Weisbach, serve as role models of how sports leaders can inspire others to perform acts of charity and kindness.

- Chairman Jerry Reinsdorf, Director of Public Relations Scott Reifert and the

Chicago White Sox organization for generously allowing special entrance to Comiskey Park in order to take photographs for this book.

- Alan Molotsky, Gerald Schur and Bill Sullivan for their insights and advice.

- Richard Magid, Marton Kander, Larry Levin and Gerald Penner for creating new opportunities.

- Ken Cooper for countless hours spent reviewing my manuscript and providing me with his critical analysis.

- Yehuda Cohen, this book's cover model, and Lewis Groner for always having the right answers to my many questions.

- Avrom Fox for instructing me on the business of selling books.

- Rabbi Pinchas Stolper for his guidance on how to reach out to Jewish youth through writing.

- Rabbi Dr. Reuven Bulka for generously allowing me to use his translation of *Ethics Of Our Fathers* from his book *Chapters of the Sages: A Psychological Commentary on Pirkey Avoth,* as the basis for all the translated references to this *Talmudic* text found in my book.

- Dr. Burton I. Cohen, Rabbi Danny Landes and Rabbi Stewart Weiss for their insights regarding the world of publishing.

- David Blachman for his outstanding photography.

- Otto and Phyllis Waldmann for their creative assistance.

- All those whose generosity helped launch this publication.

- My congregants who have provided me with beneficial feedback regarding my spiritual messages.

- The reference librarians at the Vernon Area Public Library for their valued research assistance.

- Joe Blank for proofreading my manuscript.

- My publishers Ilan Greenfield and Dror Greenfield of Gefen Publishing House, Ltd., for their patience and professionalism.

- My favorite sports teams: the Chicago White Sox, Chicago Bulls, Michigan Wolverines and Northwestern Wildcats for providing me with both entertainment and important "spiritual" material.

- Finally, to the Almighty for giving me the gift of life each day.

FOREWORD

by
Lou Weisbach and Leigh Steinberg*

Perspective is the word to describe Rabbi James Gordon's *Pray Ball! The Spiritual Insights of a Jewish Sports Fan.*

Leafing through the pages of this thought-provoking book, one realizes that the world of sports can be a truly inspiring place to be — provided the hours spent playing or watching are put to good use. A gifted athlete who donates his time and money back to the community and who understands the value of his fellow human being has a proper perspective.

Through this compilation of inspirational messages, Gordon connects sports with Jewish tradition. The stories and analogies he uses focus on how we should conduct ourselves as individuals and with each other.

Respect, sportsmanship, leadership, team play and even physical fitness are all examples of lessons we learn in Judaism which can be directly applied in sports.

---

* **Lou Weisbach** is the Founder and President of HA•LO Industries, Inc., the leader in the promotional products industry. The son of a renowned Rabbi, Weisbach was formerly the basketball coach of Chicago's Ida Crown Jewish Academy.

Leigh Steinberg is widely recognized as America's leading sports attorney, representing many of the world's top athletes. Steinberg served as technical advisor for the films *Jerry Maguire* and *Any Given Sunday.*

Both Weisbach and Steinberg are well known for their philanthropic endeavors.

How does the coaching genius of Phil Jackson teach the Jewish concept of Family Harmony (*Shalom Bayit*)? What moral responsibility, as "my brother's keeper," does a sports agent have to his client? How does the relationship between Tiger Woods and his father reflect Jewish values? What do we learn about *teshuva* — repentance — from Dennis Rodman?

These are all questions which put the games we play and watch into proper perspective.

We all remember what it was like to watch Michael Jordan flying through the air. We had the opportunity to admire more than just one of the greatest athletes of our time. We saw a *mensch* — a proper human being. A role model for kids, even today, and an example — on and off the court — of how we should conduct ourselves. We should all try to *be like Mike.*

Leadership, philanthropy, sportsmanship, fair play are all lessons we learn from our Jewish tradition. *Pray Ball! The Spiritual Insights of a Jewish Sports Fan* combines the best of both the sports and Jewish worlds.

INTRODUCTION

When I was five years old, I attended my first professional sporting event, a Chicago White Sox game. I fell in love with baseball and was introduced to an exciting new world. I became an avid fan, frequented the ball park, purchased my first baseball mitt, and played catch almost every day with my father and friends. My interest soon evolved into practicing my rudimentary reading and mathematics skills by reading the sports pages of the daily newspaper. (To this day, I still read the sports section first!) Along with marking *Shabbat* (the Sabbath) and the seasonal holy days on my calendar, I still acknowledge the seasons of the year with their corresponding sports.

My story is not unique. It is rather typical of many American Jews. How many of us associate *Yom Kippur,* the most awesome day of the year, with the World Series — for many, the most awesome championship of the year? How many of us associate Passover, the festival of freedom, with the NBA playoffs or the beginning of the baseball season?

> "For everything there is a time and there is a season for everything under the heaven."
>
> (*Ecclesiastes* 3:1)

These are the words of King Solomon, first stated almost 3,000 years ago. Every action, reaction and emotion has its appropriate time and season. The words of *Ecclesiastes (Kohelet)* were heeded not only by the Jewish people, but its universal lessons were followed by the non-Jewish world as well. Everything we do has its designated time or season. As individuals, we celebrate births, *Bar* and *Bat Mitzvahs,* funerals and other life cycle events at their appropriate times and seasons. As a people, we celebrate our holidays according to the seasons of the year. Passover is the holiday of the spring time, while the High Holy Days are in the fall.

"...vanity of vanities, everything is vanity!"

(*Ecclesiastes* 1:2)

King Solomon teaches us that without a spiritual connection, all of our activities are futile. An involvement in sports, both as a spectator and participant, can provide a deeper inner-meaning into our lives. For me, sports has emphasized such important traditional Jewish lessons as cooperation (team play), respect (sportsmanship), hard work and understanding our own limitations.

As a Rabbi, I am faced with the constant challenge to inspire others to excel in their spiritual endeavors: to follow the ways of the *Torah*, our tradition, our way of life. *Pray Ball! The Spiritual Insights of a Jewish Sports Fan* is a celebration of sports as it relates to Jewish tradition. It is my attempt to blend together two of my greatest passions: Judaism and sports, prayer and ball. This book is my attempt to spiritually connect with the sports fan.

Pray Ball! is comprised of a series of spiritual messages pertaining to eight sports-related topics: baseball, basketball, the Olympics, hockey, football, golf, sports agency, and leaders and heroes. Many of these messages are modified versions of sermons which I composed. Each of the book's chapters is introduced by a phrase from *Ecclesiastes*, connecting the sport with its most appropriate "Solomonic" season. In order to reach out to a diverse audience, I have included an extensive glossary of Jewish terms and personalities mentioned in this book.

I sincerely hope that the spiritual insights provided in this book will inspire others to apply greater meaning to even the most ordinary events of their life, thereby elevating their own level of observance and spirituality.

— Rabbi James M. Gordon, J.D.

Buffalo Grove, Illinois
September 1, 1999
20 *Elul* 5759

CHAPTER 1

BASEBALL
A Season for Being Born

"A season to be born..."
(*Ecclesiastes* 3:2)

The spring is a time of rebirth. It is the season when flowers bloom, the buds of trees begin to open and a time when many birds return home from their warm southern climates. It is also the time for baseball.

For many American "Baby Boomers," baseball was the first sport to which we were introduced both as fans and participants. It was the season into which we were born for the roles of sports participant and spectator.

Pray Ball!

Take Me Out to the *Minyan*

On my first day as a full-time pulpit Rabbi, I was greeted by the sad news that Mr. Edward Weksler, one of my senior congregants, had passed away. Later that day I met with Mr. Weksler's son Mark, also a synagogue member. In our discussions, Mark, an only child, asked me about the opportunity to recite *Kaddish* in our community. I responded that, at that time, our synagogue did not have a daily *minyan*. In fact, no synagogue in our area provided this service.

Mark looked at me and said firmly, but respectfully, "Rabbi, that is unacceptable."

Mark was right. It was unacceptable. A regular daily *minyan* is a major cornerstone of all Jewish communities. A *minyan* provides the opportunity for Jewish people to congregate together on a daily basis and deliver the most powerful type of prayer. Only when there is a gathering of at least ten Jewish men can a mourner recite the *Kaddish*. Only when there is a *minyan* can the *Torah* be read. A Jewish community which does not have a regular *minyan* is comparable to an opera without a tenor, a meal without bread, a corporation without a CEO, a major American city without a professional baseball team. A Jewish community is simply only a community without a daily *minyan*.

Veteran congregants told me that attempts to organize a regular *shul minyan* had been tried, but were unsuccessful. How were we going to disprove the "non-believers" and establish a regular daily *minyan*? Mark and I, with the support of many others, eventually succeeded in this magnanimous goal and we developed our *minyan*.

The Hebrew expression *"mi-tokh sh'lo li-sh'ma ba li-sh'ma"*[1] teaches that even if a person performs a *mitzvah* (God's commandment) for reasons other than fulfilling the actual commandment, after a while, s/he will perform it for the right (religious) reason. In this regard, our community was no different than most other American Jewish communities. In our community it simply was not enough to announce that we needed a *minyan*, and men would line up each day to ensure the quorum. Like similarly situated communities, we needed to be creative in our marketing approach.

In the early stages, we tried *minyan phon-a-thons, appeals*, (infomercial) *minutes,* and special *minyan letters*. We also were very deliberate in selecting the times for *minyanim*. To enable participants to travel to downtown Chicago and other distant locations, we knew that our morning *Shaḥarit minyan* had to be completed by about 7:00 a.m. each day. The logical starting times, therefore, were either 6:10 a.m. or 6:15 a.m. When I recommended these times, the response was that these were "un-Godly" hours. I then suggested that we begin each morning at 6:13. What could be more "Godly" than starting at 6:13 (*Taryag*) the total number of *mitzvot* (613) as ordained in the *Torah*? Nobody could reject this starting time. Slowly, little by little, we were getting closer to our magic number ten, but we had not reached it yet.

One day, during an informal conversation with several lay leaders of my synagogue, one of us suggested half jokingly, "How about giving away baseball tickets? Maybe that will bring them in?" The rest, as they say, is history. A new idea was born: *Take Me Out to the Minyan.*

For the next three years, during the summer months, we encouraged daily *minyan* attendance through the *Take Me Out to the Minyan* incentive program. For each early morning *minyan* attended, a participant received two innings of credit. For all other *minyanim*, a participant received one inning of credit. Once a participant received nine innings credit, he was entitled to a complimentary outing to a professional baseball game. The program instilled great hope and enthusiasm. *Take Me Out to the Minyan* was a program which indeed could inspire its participants to proudly proclaim: *Pray Ball!*

Many parallels exist between a *minyan* and baseball. Each activity demands a basic number of participants. According to the American League, which follows the Designated Hitter's Rule, ten players are needed. A *minyan* requires a minimum of ten Jewish men. In both baseball and a *minyan*, each participant individually plays an important role. However, to be effective in either activity, all participants must participate as a group and give their maximum "team effort." Similar to praying (*davening*) and playing baseball, the more spirited the group, usually the more successful the group. Finally, in a best-of-both worlds scenario, *minyan* and baseball become one and the same when — as in Oriole Park at Camden Yards in Baltimore and New York's Shea Stadium — there is, I have heard, a daily *minyan* during the seventh inning stretch in one of the concession rooms!

For many years now, baseball has been considered the "American Pastime." It was our hope, as in all successful Jewish communities, that a regular daily *minyan* would become the "pastime" of our community. Although we knew many "curve balls" would be thrown our way while "pitching" our *minyan*, we were confident that we would not "strike out."

The only remaining obstacle was how to finance the *Take Me Out to the Minyan* program. After all, not only were we providing each participant with a complimentary ticket to a professional baseball game, but a bag dinner and round trip transportation! Our total cost per person was about $20.

Every successful sports team needs a fan club. With that precedent in mind, we created the *Take Me Out to the Minyan Fan Club*. Membership was $9 (one-half of ḥai-18) and privileges included a specially inscribed leather *kippah* along with a membership card.

My wife, Marilyn, and I also wrote the lyrics to our team song, *Take Me Out to the Minyan*, sung to the hit song, *Take Me Out to the Ball Game*. The words are:

> Take me out to the *minyan*,
> Take me out to the *shul*.
> Buy me a *kippah* and a pair of *tefillin*,
> My parents will be smiling and *qvellin'*.
> Let us *daven* and *layne* with *kavana*,
> If we don't hit ten what a *shanda*.
> For it's ten, not eight, nor nine men,
> That make a *minyan*!

The *Take Me Out to the Minyan* incentive program was my first formal attempt as a Rabbi to combine two of my greatest loves, Judaism and sports.

The program was a huge success. More important than experiencing enjoyable outings to professional baseball games, we promoted the importance of having a regular daily *minyan* in our community.

Some final thoughts...

Our second *Take Me Out to the Minyan* outing took us to the new Comiskey Park, where the White Sox were scheduled to play the New York Yankees. Neither the loss suffered by the White Sox that night, nor the exceptionally long rain delays, ruined an important evening in my life. That day, August 23, 1993, marked the first birthday of my eldest child Max Newman Gordon. Although "Baby Max" spent much of the evening being strolled around the beautiful modern baseball stadium by his father, an important message was conveyed. As a father, I was passing along two important traditions to my son: *minyan* and baseball, *Pray Ball!* With a *minyan*, we connect with God and with other members of our Jewish community. With baseball, we connect with millions of members of our host American community.

Terrance Mann, a fictitious writer portrayed by actor James Earl Jones in the movie *Field of Dreams*, delivered a most inspiring soliloquy about the American tradition of baseball. Mann stressed how baseball has been a constant in this country's history and life. His words were so moving that he inspired Ray, portrayed by Kevin Costner, to continue pursuing his dream of building a baseball field in the middle of his obscure Iowa farm. This pursuit eventually led to the spiritual reconciliation between Ray and his father, John Kinsella, a minor league baseball player.[2]

In the *Book of Genesis*, God assures the Patriarch Abraham that he will be the leader of a prolific nation. In describing the great future numbers of members of the Children of Israel (*B'nei Yisrael*), two comparisons are used: "the stars of the heaven" and "the sand on the seashore."

Our Sages teach that these two analogies are symbolic of the importance of individuality as well as our connection to the community. Like the stars, we as individuals must strive to succeed and shine bright. Like the sand on the seashore, we must be cohesive and work together as a community.

The importance of striving to be like stars and sand is extremely applicable to both baseball and *davening*. When we play baseball, a sport played sometimes on sand and at times under the stars, it is important for each individual to try his hardest to achieve greatness as both a hitter and fielder. It is even more critical, however, for him to bond with his teammates in order to become a team player. Ultimately, this is the only way to succeed.

When we pray, as individuals, we must each focus and *daven* with all our might. However, our Sages still teach us that the highest level of prayer is achieved only when we gather together as a community with a *minyan*.

Mickey, Jerry, Rabbi Eliezer
and the Grateful Dead

Weread in the *Talmud*:

> Rabbi Eliezer says:
> > "Repent [Return]
> > one day before your death."

> Rabbi Eliezer's students asked him:
> > "And does a person know on which day he will die?"

> He [Rabbi Eliezer] responded:
> > "And all the more so why he should repent today;
> > perhaps he will die tomorrow. In this way, he will
> > find himself [as if he were] penitent his entire life."
> > > (*Shabbat* 153a)

In August of 1995, Jerry Garcia and Mickey Mantle died within a week of each other. Perhaps with most people their deaths conjured images of a Grateful Dead concert or of a tape measure home run, but I was focused on this particular passage from the *Talmud*. Besides the strange fact that these two super popular American figures died within only a few days of each other, what did Jerry and "The Mick" have in common? I am not aware of Mickey Mantle being a

"Deadhead" or of Jerry Garcia being a Yankee fan. I don't ever recall seeing footage of Mantle at a Grateful Dead concert or Garcia at a Yankees game!

Even though they may not have been personal friends or colleagues in the same business, Mickey Mantle and Jerry Garcia did have a lot in common. They were both unpretentious individuals who rose to stardom in their respective entertainment professions. While doing so, they remained common men — ordinary human beings. While rising to stardom, they accumulated problems that were prevalent among the common man. These problems included personal tragedies, marital difficulties and self-indulgent lifestyles that probably induced serious health problems.

Despite playing a "mean" guitar, Jerry Garcia was flawed. It took an inordinate amount of physical and emotional strength to record one hit record after the next, and to perform before one packed concert crowd after the other. To play Major League Baseball like Mickey Mantle did for eighteen injury-plagued years also took superhuman strength. In spite of a Hall of Fame career, Mickey Mantle also was flawed.

Unfortunately, both Jerry Garcia and Mickey Mantle relied on self-destructive means of support to help them through life's daily demands. Garcia depended heavily on drugs.[3] He disguised it as a recreational habit. Unfortunately, Garcia's actions helped glamorize illegal drug use to his millions of fans.

Mickey Mantle abused alcohol.[4] He did so, in part, perhaps as an escape from the stresses of being a megastar. Mantle began drinking as a 19-year-old Yankee rookie to help escape the pain he experienced from the premature death of his father to Hodgkin's Disease at age 39. A number of his close male relatives including one of his sons also died young. Mickey Mantle had good reasons to fear that he would never grow old. Why not live life to its "fullest?" Why not "eat, drink and be merry, for tomorrow you die?"[5]

After learning of Mantle's death, I was reminded of Rabbi Eliezer's quote from the *Talmud*. This teaches that the best time for repentance (*teshuva*) is every single day of our lives. After all, we do not know when we will die so we must always be ready. We must not wait until we are on our deathbeds before we realize what our mistakes are and what we must do to correct them. In this way, we must not be like Jerry Garcia and Mickey Mantle.

For Garcia and Mantle, *teshuva* came too late.

It was not until 1994 that Mickey Mantle finally admitted he was an alcoholic when he sought treatment at the Betty Ford Center. Unfortunately, however, it was simply too late. In great likelihood, the alcohol had already destroyed his liver and hastened the development and spread of his cancer.

In a 1994 *Sports Illustrated* article, Mickey Mantle quoted the sentiments of his former manager Casey Stengle:

> "This guy's going to be better than Joe DiMaggio and Babe Ruth." It didn't happen... God gave me a great body... and I didn't take care of it. And I blame a lot of it on alcohol.[6]

Mantle dedicated the "ninth inning" of his life to warning others of the evils of alcoholism. In his eulogy, broadcaster Bob Costas complimented Mantle for "the sheer grace of that ninth inning,...the simple eloquence and honesty to tell others to take heed of his mistakes."[7] Unfortunately, there were no "extra innings" for The Mick.

Jerry Garcia gave his last live concert at Chicago's Soldier Field in July, 1995. Soon after this concert, he too checked into the Betty Ford Center to try to deal with his drug and smoking addictions. He later checked into a small private clinic outside of San Francisco where he died in his sleep. After many years of drug use, Garcia also acknowledged his human frailties and broadcasted his abuse to the world. This helped warn others not to make the same mistake.

Ironically from a Jewish perspective, both Garcia and Mantle died close to two weekly *Torah* portions which make reference to the importance of caring for our health.[8] The *Torah* teaches that we must take care of our health. We must follow a proper diet, exercise appropriately and adopt proper sleep patterns. We must take this physical prescription and incorporate a proper spiritual diet into our daily lives as well. This includes a life dedicated to the study of *Torah* and the performance of *mitzvot*.

It is always important to remember the lesson of Rabbi Eliezer's quote in the *Talmud* that the best time for *teshuva* is each day of our lives. This passage highlights the Jewish legal (*Halakhic*) fact that we have the potential, with few exceptions, to perform *teshuva* for all sins which we may commit. One sin for which we can never repent in this world is murder; since only the victim can ultimately grant us forgiveness (*m'hila*) and they, of course, are no longer here. Similarly, there are several sins for which, theoretically, we can repent but for all practical purposes, we can never fully repent. One such sin is damaging a person's reputation.[9] Another sin is abusing our bodies!

Sometimes our timing may be off. We may want to change our ways, but are prevented from doing so since we have helped cause irreparable damage. We were too late. We can be our own worst enemies. This was the case with both Mickey Mantle and Jerry Garcia. Their good intentions were simply too late.

We must resolve to put into action whatever it takes for us to take better care of our health. We must heed the lessons of Jerry Garcia and Mickey Mantle and change our ways. After all, for all practical purposes, today is the day before we die. We must do all that we can to ensure that we reach the Jewish goal of living 120 years, the life span of Moses Our Teacher (*Moshe Rabbenu*): 120 years of caring not only for our physical well-being but also for our spiritual needs. Only then will we achieve the Jewish status of being — the "Grateful Dead."

2632, 613, Cal and Passion!

On September 6, 1995, Cal Ripken, Jr., broke a 58-year-old Major League Baseball record, when he appeared in his 2,131st consecutive Major League Baseball game. This astounding record of consecutive appearances spans more than 13 years and was previously held by the late, great Lou Gehrig of the New York Yankees. About three years later, on September 20, 1998, coincidentally corresponding to *Rosh Hashanah 5759*, Ripken quantified his Iron Man record. That night, the Baltimore Orioles infielder voluntarily removed his name from his team's line-up in their game against the New York Yankees. With Cal Ripken, Jr., not playing in that game against Gehrig's old team, Ripken's record for consecutive Major League Baseball games played was firmly established at 2,632.[10]

The record is a mark of endurance, durability and constancy. More than anything else, however, this record is a mark of passion; Ripken never would have achieved this feat without an intense love of and enthusiasm for the game of baseball. Without Cal Ripken's passion, Gehrig's record would still stand.

Sports is about records and breaking records. Examples include: Wilt Chamberlain scoring 100 points in a single basketball game; Pete Rose connecting with his record-breaking career hit; Hank Aaron belting his 715th career home run; and Mark McGwire and Sammy Sosa hitting their 62nd home runs of the 1998 season. Cal Ripken's record in many ways exceeds them all. His record stands out from all of these other milestones in that the primary basis of this amazing record is not necessarily strength or skill, but rather endurance, durability and constancy, traits which are all inspired and driven by passion.

How many of us can say that we have not missed a single day of work in over

16 years? How many of us work in environments where we are potentially exposed to the tremendous threats of injury like those of a Major League infielder? From May 30, 1982, when Ripken began his streak to September 20, 1998, when Ripken ended his streak — over 3,600 major league ballplayers were on the disabled list!

The comic Woody Allen once remarked that, "Eighty percent of success is showing up."[11] Critics have claimed that Ripken's feat cannot be compared to accounts of strength and skill, like Hank Aaron's career home run record or Pete Rose's career hit record. After all, basically all Ripken had to do during those 16 years was show up.

What critics overlook is the fact that showing up is not enough. In order to be selected for a starting line-up day in and day out, you have to perform at a Major League level. In order to play at a Major League level for so long, you have to play with passion. With relatively few exceptions, this is how Cal Ripken, Jr., performed during the course of these 16 years. Along the way, he set records such as committing the fewest errors ever by a Major League shortstop in one single season, and hitting the most career home runs by any Major League shortstop ever to play the game.

Critics also claim that Ripken gets paid millions of dollars to perform so he should set records! Most Major League players do get paid extremely well, but they do not have the passion exhibited by Ripken, who gives 100 percent in everything he undertakes. Whether it be in his role as a father or as a player in a pick up basketball game or signing autographs for fans, he gives his all. That is the type of guy he is. Cal Ripken, Jr., approaches every challenge in life with great passion!

The "Ripken Streak" as it was dubbed, is a story which captivated a large segment of America's sports fans. The Oriole-Angel game of September 6, 1996, was deemed so important that the U.S. Senate dismissed early that day, and both President Clinton and Vice President Gore attended the game in Baltimore. According to *Sports Illustrated*: "The Streak wasn't just his identity; it was ours, too. This was America the way we wish it to be — blue-collar, reliable, built on an honest day of work, one day after another..."[12] Ultimately, Cal Ripken's Iron Man record is about a man's passion for his work.

There are many other examples of passion in the world of sports. One such example is the passionate performance of U.S. gymnast Kerri Strug in the 1996 Summer Olympics.

On the fifth day of Olympic competition, the U.S. Women's gymnastics team was very close to out-pointing the Russian women's team and winning the Olympic gold medal in women's gymnastics team competition. Whether the U.S. team would bring home the gold depended on the performance of their final participant in the vault event — four foot nine inch Kerri Strug. On her first vault attempt, Strug — who proudly identifies as a Jew — landed on her heels and fell back leaving her with an injured leg. In spite of the severe injury she went forward with her second vault. Not only did Kerri Strug successfully complete the second vault attempt, but she earned a 9.712 score, which was high enough for her team to win the gold medal!

The story of Kerri Strug epitomizes the importance of passion.

Jewish tradition also promotes passion. Rabbi Dr. Jacob J. Schacter tells a story about how during the early years of communism in Europe, many observant Jews were misled into thinking that communism, not *Torah*, provided life's answers:

> Once, a number of *Hasidim* were sitting with their *Rebbe* and, in a sad and despondent mood, asked him, "*Rebbe*, tell us. Why is it that the communists are so successful and we are on the defensive? After all, what we have is *emes* (truth) and what they have is *sheker* (falsehood)?"
>
> Said the *Rebbe*, "Yes, my children, you are right. We have *emes* and they have *sheker*. But there is also another significant difference between us. You see, they fight for their *sheker* with *emes*, while we fight for our *emes* with *sheker*. They fight for their falsehood, but they do so with conviction, with feeling, with passion, convinced of the certainty of their position. We, on the other hand, fight for our truth, but we do so halfheartedly, in a matter of fact way, in a haphazard and perfunctory manner. We have the *emes*, no doubt about it, but in order to win the battle we need to fight for the *emes* with *emes*."[13]

In addition to reinforcing the importance of passion, this story also reminds us that as Jews we must be careful in "choosing our battles." We must *only* engage in confrontations that are endorsed by Jewish tradition, and those led by worthy, educated and informed leaders. We must not be misled by our evil inclination (*yetzer ha-ra*) and by false, ignorant leaders. We must always "fight for the *emes* with *emes*."

The *Torah*, *Talmud* and other traditional Jewish texts are replete with stories involving our heroes and how they fought with passion for true, just causes.

We read about Moses and how he fought for the well-being of Israel. On *Yom Kippur*, we read about how the Ten Martyrs displayed the ultimate in passion by giving their lives for the preservation of *Torah*. In modern history, we are reminded of the passion of *Hanna Szenes*, *Menachem Begin*, and *Yonatan Netanyahu* as they passionately fought for the creation and preservation of a Jewish Land — the modern State of Israel.

The *Torah* (*Genesis* 21) teaches about Sara's passionate but controversial decision to banish Ishmael — Abraham's son born from Hagar, the maidservant — from her home. Sara's great passion for her own son Isaac, for her faith and her desire to ensure the proper leadership of our people, led her to take such a bold action which was later endorsed by the Almighty.

In the *Book of Samuel* (*Samuel* I, 1), we read about another passionate woman, Hanna. Hanna's desire for a child led her to engage in passionate prayer; her prayer was so passionate that in many ways it serves as the model on how we must pray.

When we read of the Binding of Isaac (*Akeidat Yitzḥak*) (*Genesis* 22), we recall how Abraham showed the ultimate in passion when he displayed his willingness to sacrifice his own adult son, Isaac. Isaac, whom our Sages tell us was 36 years old at the time of the *Akeida*, also displayed the ultimate in passion by submitting to God's command willingly.

The High Holy Days are a time when we are especially keen and aware of the need for passion. In order to help ensure a healthy and successful year, we are told that we must engage in these three activities: repentance (*teshuva*), prayer (*tefilla*), and charity (*tzedaka*) — all activities which require intense passion.[14]

Maimonides teaches that the ultimate form of repentance (*teshuva*) is performed when a person fails to commit a sin, when he is confronted with the same situation that previously led him to commit that particular sin. This is what is known as perfect repentance (*teshuva g'mura*). True *teshuva* requires the penitent person to have the passion of wanting to change for the better.

When we pray, it is simply not enough to sit back and move our lips. The best prayer is one which comes from the heart. Hanna's prayer, for example, was a prayer recited with intense passion and fervor (*kavana*).

Likewise, according to Maimonides, the highest level of *tzedaka* is not simply taking out a checkbook and writing a check. Rather, it requires us to do something to help the person in need become self-sufficient:

> There are eight levels of charity, each one higher than the other. The highest level, for which there is none greater, is when one strengthens the hand of a poor Jew and gives him a gift or [an] [interest-free] loan or forms a partnership with him or finds work for him in order to strengthen him so that he no longer needs to ask from other people...
>
> (Maimonides, *Mishneh Torah, Hilkhot Matanot la-Evyonim* 10:7)

The highest level of *tzedaka* requires us to act passionately, to find a job for the person who is in need, to give him an interest-free loan, to act in a way that will make him feel like a *mensch*.

Throughout the year, we are taught that a key to our success is having passion in performing just and true causes. This is especially stressed during the High Holy Days (*Yamim Noraim*). At that time, and at all times, we must show God our passion through prayer, the study of *Torah* and the performance of the **613** *mitzvot*.

We must show our families our passion not only by providing them with their material needs, but by spending Jewish Quality Time with them. We must show passion to our Jewish communities here and in Israel by supporting their worthy efforts. Ultimately, however, we must show ourselves that we are capable of choosing the right causes and fighting passionately for them.

What causes are worth fighting for? What causes are worth being passionate about? Here are some of my choices for passionate causes worth fighting for:

1. *Family.* We must fight passionately for the physical and spiritual well-being of our families.

2. *Jewish Education.* We must be passionate in providing comprehensive day school education, not only for our own children and grandchildren, but for all Jewish children.

3. *Israel.* We must be passionate in our support of those living in Israel and in the fight for a secure Jewish state with the undivided capital of Jerusalem. It must be a country with safe and secure borders, a country which is the world leader in *Torah* education for all Jews, and a homeland for our brethren in peril. It must be a state which is the world leader in the development of science, medicine and technology.

4. *Synagogues/Jewish Community.* We must be willing to fight to ensure the strength of the synagogue and the Jewish community. By ensuring the proper training and development of top Jewish community professionals and lay leaders, we must fight passionately to develop and strengthen synagogues and other Jewish community organizations.

5. *Survival of the Jewish People.* We must be passionate in clearly expressing to our children and grandchildren the importance of preserving our heritage and traditions. The most effective way to do this is by structuring a Jewish environment and making available a traditional Jewish education for all Jews.

6. *Justice (Tzedek).* We must passionately fight to ensure that our fellow human beings are treated fairly, kindly and with com**passion** — a form of passion.

These are some of the causes I believe are worth fighting for. What causes do you feel worthy of **your** intense passion?

From Moses to Jackie Robinson
Let Freedom Ring!

More than 30 years ago as a child growing up, one of my favorite English Passover (*Pesaḥ*) songs was *Go Down Moses*. As many of you know, the beginning words of this ballad are:

> When Israel was in Egypt's land
> Let my people go
> Oppressed so hard they could not stand
> Let my people go
> Go down, Moses, way down in Egypt land
> Tell ol' Pharaoh, let my people go[15]

Not only is this song a source of inspiration for Jews, but African-Americans have recorded it as a traditional black folk song.

> "We were slaves of Pharaoh in Egypt."
>
> (*Passover Haggadah*)

Passover is the recollection of the historical account of our slavery and redemption from Egypt. We retell the oppression we suffered at the hands of Pharaoh, and we also express our gratitude to God for the opportunity to leave Egypt.

As Jews, we share common bonds with people of all different religions, races and backgrounds. A common bond we share with African-Americans is our history of physical enslavement, our struggle for acceptance and equal treatment in the United States, and our gratitude for our progress in slowly achieving societal acceptance.

For both Jews and blacks, these messages are relevant daily. As Jews ponder these lessons around Passover time, black Americans are also focusing on these lessons especially at this time.

April 15, 1997, a week before Passover, marked the 50th anniversary of Jackie Robinson breaking the baseball color barrier when he stepped onto the diamond at Ebbets Field to play first base for the Brooklyn Dodgers.

When Jackie Robinson, star player of the Negro Leagues, stepped onto the field that first day in 1947, and for all practical purposes, every single day of his 10 year Major League Baseball career, he represented all blacks and other minorities who would follow Robinson's example in professional sports. More importantly, he became a "test case" for all blacks and other minorities facing work force discrimination in America.

As *New York Age* editor Ludlow Werner wrote:

> I am happy over the event, but I'm sorry for Jackie. He will be haunted by the expectations of his race. Unlike white players, he can never afford an off day or an off night. His private life will be watched too, because white Americans will judge the Negro race by everything he does...[16]

To mark the fiftieth anniversary of this historic event, the game played on April 15, 1997, between the New York Mets and Los Angeles Dodgers, was interrupted after the fifth inning for a special celebratory ceremony. Presentations were made by President Bill Clinton and then Acting Baseball Commissioner Bud Selig to Robinson's widow, Rachel. Selig honored Robinson and his life accomplishments by retiring his old uniform number 42. No player will ever again be issued uniform number 42 in Major League Baseball.

Commenting on Jackie Robinson's impact on both baseball and America, President Clinton said:

It is hard to believe that 50 years ago at Ebbets Field, a 28-year-old rookie changed the face of baseball and the face of America forever. Jackie Robinson scored the go-ahead run that day, and we have been trying to catch up ever since.[17]

The Simon Wiesenthal Center teaches the world all about the Holocaust (*Shoah*), largely by stressing that it is the most horrific example in world history of bigotry, racism and unwarranted hatred.

A feature of the Wiesenthal Center in Los Angeles, is the *Beit Hashoah* Museum of Tolerance. In 1997, a special exhibit there was one entitled, *Stealing Home: How Jackie Robinson Changed America.* A document describing this exhibit states that:

> The intention of this exhibit will be to show not only how Jackie Robinson broke the color barrier in Major League Baseball but how his courageous efforts reached beyond the sport and helped raise the social consciousness of this nation to new levels of tolerance and understanding.[18]

When we taste the bitter herbs (*maror*) at the Passover *Seder,* we are reminded of the bitter times our ancestors endured as slaves in Egypt. When we dip the vegetable (*karpas*) in the salt water, we are reminded of the tears shed by the Israelite slaves. Although sweet in taste, the apple and nut mortar-looking mixture known as ḥaroset further reminds us of the slavery experience of our forefathers.

During his baseball career, Jackie Robinson also experienced many bitter moments. Robinson did not make it to the Major Leagues until he was 28 years old. Many hardships delayed his arrival. He was nearly court-martialed while serving in the United States Army during World War II for defying orders to sit at the back of a military bus, and, along with all other black personnel in the Negro League, Robinson was consistently refused entry to "white only" restaurants and hotels.

Even in the Major Leagues, Robinson endured constant racist taunts from fans and occasional death threats. Opposing team players contemplated whether they should condone his promotion to the "big leagues" by even taking the field upon which he played. Many of Robinson's own Dodger teammates did not welcome him right away. A former Brooklyn teammate recently recalled on national radio how a number of Dodger teammates circulated a petition among fellow Dodgers protesting his signing.

Referring to Robinson's superb athletic ability, Mel Jones, Montreal general manager in the old Negro League, exclaimed, "What can't he do?... [Aside from eating] in the dining room of the Waldorf-Astoria."[19]

Because of Robinson's trailblazing courage, pride, character and superior baseball skills, two additional black players, Larry Doby and Henry Thompson, were signed into the Major Leagues later that same season. Later, in 1975, Frank Robinson became the first black man to serve as manager of a Major League Baseball team, the Cleveland Indians. In 1976, Bill Lucas was appointed the director of player personnel for the Atlanta Braves becoming the first black to act as a general manager. In 1989, Bill White was named the President of the National League, becoming the first black to serve as president of a major professional sports league.

Jackie Robinson's historic appearance over 50 years ago also led to the emergence and acceptance of black athletes and managers in other professional sports. Almost 50 years to the day after Jackie Robinson broke Major League Baseball's color barrier, a 21-year-old African-American named Tiger Woods transcended the white world of professional golf when he won the Masters Tournament with a record shattering performance.

It can also be argued that Jackie Robinson's efforts helped ease the prejudicial and anti-Semitic tensions experienced by Jews and other professional minority athletes in the 1940s. It was noted that Jackie Robinson shared a special relationship with Hall of Fame Jewish slugger Hank Greenberg. Greenberg, who was ending his career with the Pittsburgh Pirates, was one of the first opposing players to openly show his support for Robinson.[20]

The achievements of Jackie Robinson — both on and off the field — are a monument to his success. In his very first Major League Baseball game on April 15, 1947, Robinson scored the winning run in the Dodgers 5-3 victory over the Boston Braves. That same year, he was chosen the National League Rookie of the Year and in 1949, he was selected as the National League's Most Valuable Player. After his retirement in 1962, Robinson was elected on the first ballot to the Major League Baseball Hall of Fame. Even during his retirement, Robinson continued his crusade for equality by devoting his time promoting civil rights and the importance of education. He worked closely with civil rights leaders Rosa Parks and Dr. Martin Luther King, Jr. In 1972, at the age of 53, Jackie Robinson succumbed to diabetes.

The legacy of Jackie Robinson transcends baseball and transcends blacks and whites as individuals. Ultimately, its impact upon America and the civil rights of each of its citizens illustrates that, in spite of all of our differences, we are very similar and we must learn to put aside our differences and co-exist in peace.

During the *Kiddush* and *Amidah* prayers, we refer to Passover as the season of our freedom (*"z'man ḥeiruteinu"*). The experience of Egypt reminds us of how vital both physical and spiritual freedom is for the Jewish people. Today, more than 50 years after Jackie Robinson first took the field for the Brooklyn Dodgers, we are especially reminded of how important freedom is — for all humankind, at all times. From Moses to Jackie Robinson — let freedom ring!

The Value of a Good Name (*Shem Tov*) in Jewish Tradition

> Rabbi *Shimon* says: There are three crowns: the crown of *Torah*, the crown of priesthood, and the crown of royalty, but the crown of a good name is superimposed on them all.
>
> (*Ethics of Our Fathers* 4:17)[21]

Our most important asset is something which is not tangible. Our most important commodity is our good name — our reputation. The way that we achieve and later preserve our good name is through our everyday deeds.

In Jewish tradition, the formula we follow to best attain and maintain a good name (*shem tov*) is by observing God's commandments (the *mitzvot*). These include observing both those *mitzvot* between a Jew and God (*mitzvot bein adam la-Makom*) as well as those between fellow human beings (*mitzvot bein adam la-ḥaveiro*).

From the *Book of Samuel I* (25:25) we learn that a person is representative of their name ("*ki khi-sh'mo ken hu*"). One of the main themes of *The Book of Ruth* (*Megilat Rut*) which we read on the festival of *Shavuot* is the importance of achieving and preserving a good name. Every name in *The Book of Ruth* has a meaning which is pertinent to the bearer of the name. For example, Ruth (*Rut*) means "to shake" ("*l'ra-tet*"). In Hebrew, we sometimes refer to an observant Jew as a person who shakes, figuratively and sometimes literally from the fear of God. Our ideal role model of a God-fearing Jew is Ruth the Moabite who, on her very own and with no ulterior motive, converted to Judaism. Ruth is a shining example of a person who possessed a good name.[22]

The importance of attaining and maintaining a good name is a key to success in all societies and in all disciplines. The success of a doctor depends on his professional reputation. Is he a good diagnostician? Does he have a pleasant bedside manner? Is he known as a successful healer? The success of a business depends on its reputation to the consuming public. Are its employees efficient? Are they pleasant? Is the product or service rendered high in quality?

Our Sages teach that a good name is even more valuable than good oil (*"Tov shem mi-shemen tov"*). When one tarnishes his good name (*shem tov*), he ends up bringing **shame** to that name.

The products and services that a professional provides is not always enough for him to succeed. In many instances, a professional's reputation as a human being is also taken into account. Such is the case, at times, in the world of sports.

Although it is unrealistic to expect athletes and other sports figures to serve as role models regarding their off-the-field behavior, it is far more realistic to judge them for their on-field performance. In certain instances, the lack of ethical behavior by sports figures can destroy their professional careers. This has been the case throughout the history of American sports.

One of the most notorious examples of self-destruction of a good name was the case of the 1919 Chicago White Sox. The White Sox, the powerhouse of the American League and favored by many to beat the Cincinnati Reds in the World Series, ended up losing. It later was alleged that gamblers had influenced eight of the Sox players by offering bribes to them to throw the World Series. These eight players were later indicted, and in 1921 tried for the activities for which they were accused. The good names (*shemot tovim*) of these eight White Sox players were **shamed**, leading them to be referred to by the public as the "Black Sox."[23] All eight players, because of their alleged involvement in this scandal, were banished for life from Organized Baseball by Commissioner Judge Kenesaw Mountain Landis.

The most famous of these players was "Shoeless Joe" Jackson. (History later noted that he may have been improperly implicated in the scandal). "Shoeless Joe" was a hero to his many fans:

As Jackson departed from the Grand Jury room, a small boy

clutched at his sleeve and tagged along after him. "Say it ain't so, Joe," he pleaded, "Say it ain't so."[24]

The sports world wishes it could say, "it ain't so," regarding post-1919 acts of **shame**, however, this unfortunately is not the case. Since that time, **shame**ful acts have been committed by many sports figures.

Perhaps the most notorious gambling allegations brought in the sports world since 1919 were the charges leveled against Cincinnati Reds manager, Pete Rose. In 1989, this Cincinnati hometown legend, without admitting to any wrongdoing, was banished for life from Major League Baseball. After a thorough investigation, Major League Baseball Commissioner Dr. Bart Giamatti had strong reason to believe that Rose was betting on baseball while serving as Reds manager.

It didn't matter that Pete Rose was the all-time "Hit King" of Major League Baseball, and it did not make a difference that Rose, known as "Charlie Hustle," inspired many to try even harder in every endeavor. By being banished for life from Major League Baseball, Rose's good name was severely damaged. The damage was so severe that the Baseball Hall of Fame, according to a rule passed in 1991, cannot even consider Rose or any other candidate on Baseball's Ineligible List. Rose still lobbies to have his life-sentence commuted to time already served, and once again be considered for admission into Baseball's Hall of Fame.

In a 1997 *Sports Illustrated* article,[25] it was recommended that the 1991 Hall of Fame eligibility rule be amended to allow banished players like Rose admission to the Hall of Fame. By doing this, Rose's stellar good name as a player will be honored without jeopardizing baseball's reputation.[26]

Other sports figures whose good names have been damaged include former football great O. J. Simpson, former Dodgers executive Al Campanis who passed away in 1998, the late broadcast analyst Jimmy "The Greek" Snyder, and golfer Fuzzy Zoeller. Campanis, Snyder and Zoeller made seemingly racist remarks which severely tarnished their good names.[27]

In the world of sports, stellar "on-field" or "on-mike" performance in and of itself is not always enough. One's success is also contingent upon preserving a good reputation, a good name.

As Jews, our good name involves how we relate with each other and how we relate with God. When we die, the only thing that remains is our reputation, our name. If we live with distinction, then we leave behind us a *shem tov*. If we live a life filled with **shame**, the opposite holds true.

An important ingredient in achieving and preserving a good name is incorporating the wonderful and positive lessons taught to us by our parents, grandparents, and other loved ones into our everyday lives. These influences, along with lessons learned from the exemplary lives of our great historical heroes, help us achieve our own *shem tov* and preserve their good names by perpetuating their stellar reputations for years to come.

We should strive to incorporate the teachings of our loved ones, along with the lessons taught by Ruth and the other Jewish heroes and martyrs. By remembering them, we preserve and perpetuate their good reputations for eternity.

> "...but the crown of a good name (*shem tov*) is superimposed on them all."
>
> (*Ethics of Our Fathers* 4:17)

Sasson v'Simḥa (Joy & Happiness)
Of Home Runs & Succot

The late Bill Veeck, former owner of the Chicago White Sox, Cleveland Indians and St. Louis Browns, was regarded as **the** master sports promoter. Veeck concocted numerous promotions to draw people to baseball games. Although many of these fans were originally attracted by such *shtick*, after a while, they slowly began to enjoy the actual game of baseball itself.

I think that even the late Mr. Veeck would agree that ultimately, the best way to attract fans is through exceptional on-field performance. Exceptional performance can include superior team play or simply the excitement generated by an individual player. This is the most direct way to cultivate happy, joyful feelings among fans.

The 1998 baseball season was filled with many exciting and joyful moments. They included: the Yankees American League record for team victories, David Wells' perfect game, Cal Ripken, Jr., voluntarily snapping his Iron Man record and Kerry Wood's record-tying 20 strikeouts in one game. It was a season regarded by some authorities as "The Greatest Season Ever."[28]

Former American League Cy Young Award Winner and Cub broadcaster Steve Stone, who proudly identifies as a Jew, referred to the 1998 baseball season as a "renaissance year." In his words, "This year, baseball put away all of the ill feelings that some of the fans had from the '94 (strike-shortened) season..."[29]

The Hebrew word for joy is *sasson*. The 1998 baseball campaign was filled with great joy and happiness. What truly made this year a **season of *sasson*** was the excitement generated by Sammy Sosa and Mark McGwire pursuing one of baseball's most coveted records: Roger Maris' 61 home runs in a single season. It was a time of joy for baseball fans because of the camaraderie these two rivals openly expressed for each other.

When McGwire hit his 62nd home run in St. Louis on September 8th while playing the Cubs, Sosa embraced his dear friend and when Sosa hit his 62nd homer the next week, through all his joy Sosa remembered McGwire, "Mark, you know I love you. It's been unbelievable. I wish you could be here with me today. I know you are watching me, and I know you have the same feeling for me as I have for you in my heart."[30]

It only makes sense that Sosa exudes love and great joy; after all, in Hebrew *sos* means to "bring joy." Sammy Sosa has brought great joy to millions of adulant baseball fans.

Sosa's "rival," the "friendly giant" Mark McGwire, also radiates love and joy. Both Sosa and McGwire are very charitable. Through the Mark McGwire Foundation, the Cardinals slugger donates a million dollars a year to benefit sexually abused children. When Hurricane Georges ravaged parts of his Dominican Republic homeland, Sosa spearheaded a relief effort for the victims of this disaster. McGwire shares a very close bond with his son and Cardinal bat boy, Matt. Sosa is also a very dedicated family man. *Sports Illustrated* recently reported that, "There's no player in baseball who mentions his wife, mother, siblings and cousins in interviews more often than the 29-year-old Sosa does."[31]

McGwire's baseball statistics have reflected his contentment in his personal life. He is happy. His personal joy about who he is and his special role as a father have helped propel him to his awesome feats on the baseball field. In many ways, he is a sports manifestation of the *Talmudic* maxim (*Ethics of Our Fathers* 4:1), "Who is rich? One who rejoices in one's portion..."[32]

In 1998, Mark McGwire and Sammy Sosa attracted fans to the ballpark, simply because of the sheer joy and happiness of the game. *Shtick* was not needed.

In their efforts to attract constituents, many times American Jewish leadership, this author included, has resorted to the "*shtick* mentality." We often rely on creative marketing to lure more Jews to join synagogues and to participate in traditional Jewish activities. We create attractive membership packages, we participate in synagogue affiliation fairs... Some leaders even give away baseball tickets for *minyan* attendance![33] Jewish tradition does indeed endorse such marketing techniques, but only if the end result is to inspire more Jews to lead more active Jewish lives. As our Sages taught, a person who does the right thing but for the wrong reason, eventually will do it for the "right" reason.

What are the "right" reasons? *Sasson* (joy) and *simḥa* (happiness). Jews should observe *mitzvot* (God's commandments) not because of a reward they may receive, but rather for the sheer joy that observing tradition brings! In the words of our Sages, "Be not like servants who serve their master for the sake of receiving a reward..." (*Ethics of Our Fathers* 1:3). Rather, our attitude should reflect the words of King David, "Worship the Lord with happiness!" (*Psalms* 100:2). King David in his *Psalms* teaches that the ideal way that a Jew should lead his life is in happiness. When we perform a *mitzvah*, we should do it not because we have to, but rather because of the joy we receive when doing it.

When *Rabbi Israel Ba-al Shem Tov* (1700-1760) founded Ḥasidism, he differentiated his philosophy from that of the mainstream *Mitnagdim* by focusing on the joy of performing a *mitzvah (simḥa shel mitzvah)*. The *Ba-al Shem Tov* advocated that one should always be joyful since the greatest acts of creativity are best achieved in an environment of joy.[34] Ḥasidic Jews, the disciples of the *Ba-al Shem Tov*, enhance the importance of traditional observance and study by placing a particular emphasis on song and dance as a celebration of one's observance.

We find examples of *sasson* (joy) and *simḥa* (happiness) throughout our traditions.

- The seventh day, *Shabbat*, is a day especially devoted to joy as we celebrate God's rest from creation. This is a day spent with a particular focus on prayer, family and God.

- At the *havdala* service where we ceremoniously bid farewell to *Shabbat*, we are reminded of the important role that happiness and joy play in our lives. During this ceremony we repeat the verse:

  > "The Jews experienced light and happiness and joy and honor."
  >
  > (*Esther* 8:16)

- Under the marriage canopy (*ḥupah*) and during the week following a wedding ceremony, we shower the newlywed couple with a series of seven blessings (*sheva berakhot*). In the final blessing under the *ḥupah*, we bless God as the One "Who has created joy (*sasson*) and happiness (*simḥa*)..."

- In the Hebrew calendar, the month of *Adar* is especially known for its happiness:

> "When *Adar* begins we must increase our happiness (*simḥa*)."
>
> (*Taanit* 29a)

During this month we also celebrate the joyful festival of *Purim*.

- Regarding the holiday of *Succot*, the *Torah* commands "and you shall rejoice in your festival" ("*v'samakhta b'ḥagekha*") (*Deuteronomy* 16:14). In our prayer liturgy we refer to this holiday as "the season of our happiness" ("*z'man simḥateinu*"). After all, *Succot* is a harvest festival. At this time we thank the Almighty for His role in properly regulating the rains and providing us with such bountiful produce. Too much or too little rain can ruin our crops. We are filled with joy and happiness (*sasson v'simḥa*) when we receive the requisite amount of rain water in a timely fashion.

  During the days of the Temple, a major manifestation of such joy was expressed through participation in the Rejoicing at the Place of (Water) Drawing (*Simḥat Beit Ha-Shoeiva*) ceremony which took place on *Succot*. In addition to a water-drawing ceremony, a major part of this event was elaborate celebration. The festivities included a candle lighting ceremony and extensive singing and dancing. The joy was so magnificent that it was said, "...whoever had not seen the rejoicing at the Place of (Water) Drawing had never witnessed happiness in his life" (*Succah* 5:1).

  Even though the Temple was destroyed almost 2,000 years ago, many communities today still mark the water libation tradition through enhanced holiday celebrations. Additionally, we express our great joy on *Succot* by blessing the *lulav* and *etrog*, dwelling in our *succot* (booths), enjoying our *succah* guests and reciting each day the *Hallel* verses from *Psalms*.

- After *Succot*, at the very end of the fall holiday season, we observe *Simḥat Torah*, a day on which we celebrate the completion and beginning of the annual cycle of *Torah* readings.

Both the 1998 Major League Baseball season and the over-3,000 year old *Succot* season share a common theme of joy and happiness. In Jewish tradition, we combine *sasson* (joy) with *simḥa* (happiness). In 1998, the baseball world achieved a sports version of *sasson v'simḥa* by bringing together Sosa and McGwire. Sammy Sosa and Mark McGwire remind us that the best reason to appreciate the sport of baseball is because of the sheer joy it can bring the participant. Likewise, the ideal reason to appreciate Judaism is because of the sheer joy and happiness it brings the one who adheres to its practices.

CHAPTER 2

BASKETBALL

A Season for Dancing

"...a season to dance."
(*Ecclesiastes* 3:4)

The flight of Michael "Air" Jordan taking off from the top-of-the-key, twisting and turning in mid-air, and landing only after first slam-dunking the ball is as close to an acrobatic dance as anyone will ever see in the sports arena.

Group Dreams

In 1994, one of the best movies of the year, one almost entirely overlooked by the Academy Awards, was a documentary entitled *Hoop Dreams*.

Hoop Dreams tells the story of a dream shared by two black African-American youth from the inner city of Chicago, Arthur Agee and William Gates. Their dream is to play in the National Basketball Association, the NBA. It is also a dream shared by their moms, dads, brothers and sisters. It is a dream shared by thousands of young men across America, many of whom are youth from the poverty stricken inner city of American metropolitan areas. Their dream is a "Group Dream." The chances of achieving their dreams are, at best, a long shot for each of these dreamers. *Time Magazine* movie reviewer Richard Corliss writes: "Making it to the NBA: It's the worst dream a boy can have. Even if he's one of the 50,000 or so high school phenoms in a year, his chances are only one in 2,000 that he will play NBA Basketball."[1]

The movie follows the lives of William and Arthur for five years, portraying their successes and failures as they pursue their dream. Arthur and William are typical of thousands of other similarly situated youth exploited by a system which, on far too many occasions, fails to adequately prepare these talented young men for alternatives to a career in professional basketball.

Dreams. In the words of musician Billy Joel, "Everybody has a dream." Sometimes we dream impossible dreams. Some dreamers are inspired by technicolor dream coats, while still others have fields of dreams. Yet we all have dreams. Dreams can give us goals, hope and comfort. Dreams can also be shattered. Other dreams can provide a vision, a direction or a path to follow in order to fulfill our dreams.

A dream can be self-centered or it can involve a larger group. We have Group Dreams for our immediate family, our extended family — the World Jewish Community (*K'lal Yisrael*), our brethren who live in Israel, and for all humanity. These are all groups for whom we dream Group Dreams. Sometimes our dreams are simple. Sometimes they contain great vision.

Perhaps the most famous contemporary Group Dream was one which provided extraordinary vision. This was the one proclaimed by the late, highly respected African-American leader, Dr. Martin Luther King, Jr.

In his efforts to promote civil rights and racial equality, Dr. King was joined in his work by people of all races, religions and ages. Included in this group were Rabbis and other Jewish community leaders.

On August 28, 1963, Reverend King delivered his famous "I Have A Dream" speech on the steps of the Lincoln Memorial in Washington, D.C. This dream remains a visionary one shared by many groups, including blacks and enlightened whites. This message promotes the importance of freedom and equality among all human beings. The theme of this most inspiring speech was articulated by such great American leaders as President Abraham Lincoln and the framers of the United States Constitution. Dr. King noted at the outset of this most powerful message that this dream continues to develop as it has not even now been fully implemented. Reverend King's speech is a Group Dream filled with great vision.[2]

For the late Dr. Martin Luther King, Jr., as well as for President Abraham Lincoln and many Jewish and other religious leaders, a major dream was and continues to be equality and freedom. This includes freedom of religion, freedom of association, and non-discrimination in schools and in places of employment.

The *Torah* is filled with dreams. There are the dreams of Jacob, Joseph, Pharaoh, the Pharaoh's chief wine steward and the Pharaoh's chief baker.

Professor Nehama Leibowitz, of blessed memory, one of the greatest traditional Biblical scholars of this generation, writes in her book *Studies In Bereshit (Genesis)* that in the *Book of Genesis* there are two basic types of dreams through which the Almighty communicates to the Jewish people and their leaders. One type of dream is that which God communicates directly to the dreamer. The second type is when the communication from God to the dreamer is done through a medium presented in the dream.[3]

Jacob's famous dream of the ladder is a dream where God communicates directly to the dreamer (and to the Jewish people). Jacob dreamt this dream the night before he left Israel, while fleeing from the wrath of his twin brother Esau:

> And he dreamt, and behold there was a ladder grounded in the earth and its top reached towards the heaven; and behold angels of God were ascending and descending on it.
>
> (*Genesis* 28:12)

Two of the leading analyses/interpretations of this dream explain that the message in Jacob's dream was not a private one exclusively for Jacob, but eventually a message for all Jewish people. Jacob's dream was a Group Dream, a Jewish Group Dream.

According to the traditional commentator *Rashi*, the ladder represents the journey of Jacob, and the angels ascending the ladder represent the angels of God who accompanied Jacob while he was in Israel. The angels descending the ladder represent the Divine angels who would accompany Jacob through his journey and stay in the Diaspora. Jacob's Group Dream tells us that as long as we, World Jewry of all generations, practice our faith, God will accompany us wherever we live.

There is, according to this interpretation, special consideration given to Jews living in Israel. This is illustrated by the angels ascending Jacob's ladder, all of whom refuse to descend it.

According to one analysis of the dream (*Midrash Tanḥuma*), Jacob's ladder represents the ladder of Jewish history. God is at the top of the ladder to help ensure not only Jacob's survival, but the eternal survival of the Jewish people. The angels of God represent the non-Jewish nations of the world. Throughout history these nations have risen and fallen. Despite their fluctuations in numbers the Jewish people, with the help of the Almighty, have survived. As long as Jacob did his part, God would protect him. Similarly, as we the Jewish people do our part in every generation, the Almighty will protect us and help ensure our existence.

Jacob's dream provided him with direction, hope and comfort. It provided a vision for the Jewish people regarding its future survival and the importance of the Land of Israel (*Eretz Yisrael*). Jacob's dream was indeed a Group Dream, a Jewish Group Dream.

We all have dreams. What are your dreams? What dreams do you have for yourself? As a parent? As a spouse? As a child? As a friend? What are your Group Dreams? For your family? For your synagogue? For your people? For Israel? For all humankind?

Here are some of my Group Dreams.

I have a dream that one day we will eliminate assimilation. Jews will marry other Jews not because they feel that they have to, but because they realize the beauty of our religion and the importance of preserving it.

I have a dream that one day all Jewish children will attend Jewish day schools, and that a Jewish day school education will be easily affordable for all families.

I have a dream that all Jewish adults will be enrolled in adult Jewish education programs, and that we will all be more open to incorporating greater *teshuva*, Jewish change and growth, into our own lives.

I have a dream that we will never, ever forget the six million Jews who perished in the Holocaust (*Shoah*), and that in their memories, we dedicate ourselves to a life filled with the study of *Torah* and its teachings.

I have a dream that we will abandon the promotion and practice of unwarranted hatred (*sinat ḥinam*), *lashon ha-ra* and other verbal sins. I have a dream that we will practice more love of our fellow Jews (*ahavat Yisrael*), and we will treat one another more kindly at all times, in our homes, and in our social and work environments.

I have a dream that someday soon the modern State of Israel will develop into a country which will be self-sufficient, and one which is not dependent upon foreign aid. I have a dream that Israel will always remain a Jewish state highly influenced by Jewish law and tradition...a country with safe, secure borders...a country with a strong military...a state with Jerusalem as its undivided capital... a country that will emerge as the world leader in developing cures for such diseases as cancer and AIDS.

I have a dream that all Jews will raise their levels of charitable giving (*tzedaka*).

I have a dream that we will search more within ourselves for blame, before we point our fingers so readily at others.

I have a dream that we will all be blessed with good health.

And finally, I have a dream that there will be a true, lasting peace in Israel and worldwide.

Everybody has a dream. Sometimes we dream impossible dreams. Some dreamers are inspired by technicolor dream coats, while others have fields of dreams. We all have dreams. Dreams can give us goals, hope and comfort. Dreams can be shattered. Dreams can provide vision.

What are your dreams?

The Menorah
A Symbol of Team Play[4]

The classic commentator *Rashi* teaches that the *Menorah* or candelabrum in the Holy Temple (*Beit ha-Mikdash*) had two unique features.[5] We learn that the entire structure of the *Menorah* was built ("hammered") from one single ingot of gold and that the six outer lights all pointed towards the center stem. The commentator known as the *S'forno*[6] further teaches that all seven lights glowed together in a way which illuminated the Israelites with a special spiritual radiance from the heavens.

The *Menorah* is symbolic of the Jewish people and their success. Like candles, each of us is radiant, talented and shining in our own way. Some are gifted doctors while others are gifted lawyers. Others are athletes and others are artists. Ultimately, we — like the *Menorah* — are all formed from the same mold. We cannot, however, truly be successful as a people unless we unite our talents like the candles of the *Menorah* and direct our energies towards a unifying force. For the Jewish people, that unifying force is the *Torah* and its teachings as transmitted by our Rabbis and other teachers of *Torah*.

In promising the Patriarchs (*Avot*) that their descendants would be numerous, the Almighty made two analogies. The great number of future Israelites are compared to "the stars in the heavens" and "the sand on the seashore." Like stars in the heavens, each Jewish person has the potential to be a unique individual. However, in order to be successful as a people we must unite and be as cohesive as the sand on the beach. This is the message of the *Menorah*, the value of team play.

The *Menorah's* message for success can be adapted by any organization, whether it is a corporation, or a professional sports team. In order to succeed, the leaders must be able to motivate the members of the group to use the best of their individual talents for the good of the team.

In successfully motivating his players, Phil Jackson, head coach of the Chicago Bulls (1989-1998), led his team to six NBA Championships.

Like the *Menorah* of the Temple days, a basketball team also has multiple branches. These branches include twelve players, a head coach and his coaching staff, the team ownership, and management. Each branch represents individual talent. However, in order to be of championship quality, it is critical that the entire team be cut from the same mold and have one common objective. In professional basketball, that objective is to win an NBA Championship.

If we were to limit the *Menorah* of the Chicago Bulls to seven branches, I would identify the six outer branches as the starting five and sixth man. I would designate the center branch as the leadership of the team represented by its coaches and team management.

Like the six outer candles of the *Menorah*, each of the top six Bulls players glows individually. By virtue of being an NBA starter, or sixth man, these players distinguish themselves as the elite among the elite. Each of these players were usually stars in college and, with few exceptions, at all levels of basketball competition.

Like the *Menorah*, the Bulls blend especially well together as a team. They are "hammered" from one piece, and follow the lead of their coaches and other management team members in setting aside their differences and committing their efforts to winning. The Bulls players learned to dedicate themselves in the ways necessary to ensure the success of champions.

These six players represent the six outer branches of the *Menorah*. The middle branch represents the coaching staff, owners and management. These forces combine to comprise the team's leadership and its commitment to winning.

The coaching staff was headed by Phil Jackson. Jackson is an extremely bright, well-read and analytical man. The son of ministers, a student of Native American Indian culture and Zen Buddhism, as well as an environmentalist, he brings a unique perspective to coaching. A student of the late legendary NBA Coach Red Holzman, Jackson is especially sensitive to the importance of a strong defense and selfless team effort in order to achieve success.

The Bulls organization is owned by a group of investors. The spokesman for this group is Chairman Jerry Reinsdorf. Reinsdorf is himself a successful attorney and businessman. He has applied his professional knowledge to help mold the Chicago Bulls to become a winning team, both on the basketball court as well as in the financial world. He has done so by being hands-on only when necessary, and otherwise delegating responsibilities.

One of the primary people to whom Reinsdorf delegates responsibility is the Bulls Vice President of Basketball Operations, Jerry Krause. Known as a tireless and loyal executive, Krause has a keen awareness of player talents and is regarded as the architect of this team when it comes to selecting championship quality talent.

It is the coaches, owners and management who collectively have decided that winning is the key objective of this organization, and that this message be conveyed effectively to the players. The players, in turn, under Coach Jackson's guidance, have exchanged selfish, individual gain for selfless, team play.

The message of the *Menorah* is actually the formula for success for all areas of life, whether secular or religious. This formula can be applied to corporations, sports teams (amateur or professional), as well as to religious organizations. In order for any entity to be successful, its members must take their personal skills in which they individually shine and follow their leaders guidance to apply them to achieve their organization's objectives.

As Jews, we must strive to observe the teachings of the *Torah* to be just, educated, compassionate and God-fearing human beings. Like the candles of the *Menorah*, we are encouraged to radiate as individuals. Some Jews excel in *Torah* study, others in performing acts of kindness (*ḥesed*), while still others in praying skills (*davening*). Like the candles of the *Menorah,* it is imperative that we radiate not only with our individual talents, but also as a unified whole. We must therefore combine forces with Jews of all backgrounds to achieve our mutually shared goals as a people.

> "And this is the work of the *Menorah*, hammered (from one single ingot of) gold from its base to its flower adornments..."
>
> (*Numbers* 8:4)

Who Knows Five? (*Ḥamisha Mi Yodeah?*)
The Significance of Five in Jewish Tradition⁷

In *Ethics of Our Fathers (Pirkei Avot)* we read the following *mishnah*:

> Every controversy which is for the sake of Heaven will ultimately endure, but any controversy which is not for the sake of Heaven will ultimately not endure. What is the prototype of a controversy which is for the sake of Heaven? — this is the controversy between Hillel and Shammai. And what is the prototype of a controversy which is not for the sake of Heaven? — this is the controversy of *Koraḥ* and all his company.
>
> (*Ethics of Our Fathers* 5:20)

In Jewish tradition we are taught that *maḥaloket* (conflict or controversy) is bad. The only exception to this general rule is the type of *maḥaloket* which involved The School of Hillel (*Beit Hillel*) and The School of Shammai (*Beit Shammai*).

Rabbi Hillel and Rabbi Shammai, two of the greatest Rabbinic scholars of all time, actually engaged in only three *maḥalokot*. Their disciples, however, were constantly engaged in *maḥaloket*. Nonetheless, all the disputes in which they were involved were all clearly philosophical and sophisticated in nature. None were personal. After all, the schools of *Hillel* and *Shammai* were interested in fine-tuning Jewish law (*Halakha*) and making it more accessible to the general public. It is because of this desire for accessibility that the *Talmud* refers to their brand of *maḥaloket* as "for the sake of Heaven" ("*l'shem shamayim*").

This same *mishnah* teaches us that the type of *maḥaloket* that is not "for the sake of heaven" is that which involved "*Koraḥ* and all his company." *Koraḥ* and his followers all wanted to personally replace Moses and Aaron as the leaders of Israel. In that respect, *Koraḥ* and his followers were completely self-centered and their *maḥaloket* was not "for the sake of Heaven."

The Jewish people, of course, do not have the "monopoly" on *maḥaloket*. Wherever in the world you go and whatever topic you explore, one seems to always run into some sort of controversy. However, I think that I have discovered one issue in the world which is not the subject of *maḥaloket*. Everyone seems to agree that the Chicago Bulls are Number One.

By winning their fifth championship in this decade under the leadership of Coach Phil Jackson, Michael "Air" Jordan and Scottie Pippen, the Bulls have made it clear that — beyond *maḥaloket* — controversy or conflict, they are indeed the best NBA team of the '90s!

Last year after delivering my message entitled, *Who Knows Four? (Arba Mi Yodeah?): The Significance of Four in Jewish Tradition*, I mailed a copy to Bulls Chairman Jerry Reinsdorf. To my pleasant surprise, I received the following response from Mr. Reinsdorf dated July 16, 1996:

> Dear Rabbi Gordon:
>
> Thank you for your letter. I found your sermon thoroughly enjoyable. Hopefully, next year you can tell your congregation about the significance of five in the Jewish Tradition.
>
> Sincerely,
> Jerry M. Reinsdorf

So, it is with great pride and with no internal/personal *maḥaloket* that I present, *Who Knows Five? (Ḥamisha Mi Yodeah?): The Significance of Five in Jewish Tradition*.

- At the end of the Passover *Seder* we sing the song, *Who Knows One? (Eḥad Mi Yodeah?)*. While being taught the significance of numbers in Jewish tradition through this fun and educational song, we are reminded that ultimately our lives revolve around God and His Oneness.

In this same song regarding **five** we are taught:

> *Ḥamisha mi yodeah?*
>
> Who knows five?
> I know five.
> Five are the Books of the *Torah*.

- In Latin the *Torah* is known as the *Pentateuch*, which means "The **Five** Books." Similarly, in Hebrew the *Torah* is also referred to as the *Ḥumash*, which comes from the word *Ḥamesh* or *Ḥamisha* which means "**five**." The *Ḥumash* refers to *Ḥamisha Ḥumshei Torah*, the **Five** Books of the *Torah*.

- In Hebrew grammar, word forms have masculine and feminine genders. *Ḥamesh* is the feminine gender of "**five**," and *ḥamisha* is the masculine form. The word *ḥamisha* is comprised of, true to its meaning, **five** letters: *ḥet, mem, yud, shin* and *heh*.

- In Hebrew, we attach a numerical value to each Hebrew letter (*gimatriah*). The Hebrew letter which corresponds to the number "**five**" is the letter *heh*, the **fifth** letter of the Hebrew Alphabet (*Aleph-Bet*).

- The letter *heh* is also a way we represent the Divine name of *Hashem*. When we refer to our God as *Hashem*, we make reference to God as our compassionate God (*Midat ha-Raḥamim*).

- The age of **five** is a critical time for a developing child. When I was **five**, I went to my first professional sports event, a Chicago White Sox baseball game. I was so enthralled with the Sox that it led me to zealously follow baseball and other sporting events. It also further motivated me to read the game reports and the newspaper statistics regarding my favorite players and teams. This, in turn, inspired me to enjoy mathematics and reading.

  In Jewish tradition, **five** is also the age that we begin to teach our children *Torah* as documented in *Pirkei Avot*:

  > "... The age of readiness for the study of Scripture is five years..."
  >
  > (*Ethics of Our Fathers* 5:25)

When a child first enters a Jewish school and learns how to read and write, he or she learns that there are key Hebrew words each comprised of **five** letters. For example, the word *mitzvot* (God's commandments) is often spelled with **five** letters: *mem-tzadi-vav-vav-tav* (מצוות).

- The source of the *mitzvot* is the *Torah*. The final three books of the *Torah* each have five letters in their Hebrew names: *Va-Yikra (Leviticus) vav-yud-kuf-resh-aleph* (ויקרא), *Ba-Midbar (Numbers) bet-mem-dalet-bet-resh* (במדבר), and *Devarim (Deuteronomy) dalet-vet-resh-yud-mem* (דברים).

- Just as we begin to teach a child *Torah* at a young age, we also begin to teach a child how to pray (*daven*). Both *Shaḥarit, shin-ḥet-resh-yud-tav* (שחרית), the morning service, and *Maariv, mem-ayin-resh-yud-vet* (מעריב), the evening service is spelled each with **five** letters.

- As part of the curriculum for primary Jewish education, we emphasize the teaching of The Ten Commandments. On each of the two tablets there are **five** commandments. With children, particular emphasis is placed on the **fifth** commandment, honoring our parents.

- The Hebrew word *Av*, in addition to meaning "father," is also the name of a month in the Hebrew (lunar) calendar. According to the count of months as outlined in the *Torah, Av* is the **fifth** month of the year!

  Regarding the month of *Av*, the *Talmud* teaches: "When *Av* begins we must decrease our happiness" (*Taanit* 29a).

  The reason we diminish our happiness in the month of *Av* is that we commemorate *Tisha b'Av* a tragic day in our history, when both of our Holy Temples were destroyed. On *Tisha b'Av*, we read *The Book of Lamentations (Megillat Eikha)*, one of the Five *Megillot*. A unique feature of *Lamentations* is that it has **five** chapters.

- As Jews, our primary purpose in life is to serve and worship God. The word for work, service or worship is another **five**-letter word *Avoda, aleph-vet- vav-dalet-heh* (עבודה). The service and worship of God is known as *Avodat Hashem*.

  We engage in *Avodat Hashem* through both formal and informal activities. We serve and worship God formally through prayer (*Tefillah*) another **five** letter word, *tav-feh-yud-lamed-heh* (תפילה) and by reading and studying the *Torah*. On *Shabbat*, in addition to the *Maftir Aliyah*, seven men are called up to the *Torah*. In many communities, after the **fifth**, Ḥamishi *Aliyah*, a special prayer for the sick (*Mi Sh'berakh*) is recited. In this prayer, we pray that the sick be blessed with a full recovery, or in Hebrew, with a *r'fuah sh'leima*.

On *Shabbat* and holidays our service and worship of God is increased. During the festival of Passover in Israel, there are **five** days of *ḥol ha-moed*, days on which most of the holy day (*yom tov*) restrictions do not apply. Similarly, on the festival of *Succot* in the Diaspora, there are also **five** days of *ḥol ha-moed*. On the festival of *Ḥanukah* we recall both the miracle of the oil as well as the military victory of the Jewish armies led by *Mattathias* and his **five** Maccabean sons: Judah, Simon, Eliezer, Yohanan and Jonathan.

Informally, we have the opportunity to engage in *Avodat Hashem* in everything we do. As such, we use our **five** senses along with our **five** fingers on each of our hands in serving God.

- We refer to an upside down hand-shaped ornament as a *ḥamsa*, which is similar to the Hebrew word *ḥamesh*, referring to the **five** fingers of the hand. The mystical purpose of the *ḥamsa* is to guard against the evil eye (*ayin ha-ra*).

- Israel, or as it is known in Hebrew — *Yisrael*, is our Jewish homeland and is comprised of **five** letters, *yud-sin-resh-aleph-lamed* (ישראל). There are **five** types of seeds, according to the *Talmud* (*Ḥallah* 1:1), to which the Land of Israel's (*Eretz Yisrael*) agricultural produce religious laws are applicable.

- And finally, the question of "who knows **five**" may be best answered by the following **five** Bulls starters, each with **five** transliterated letters in their names:

  1. Jordan, *gimel-vav-resh-dalet-nun* (ג'ורדן);
  2. Rodman, *resh-vav-dalet-mem-nun* (רודמן);
  3. Pippen, *peh-yud-peh-yud-nun* (פיפין);
  4. Harper, *heh-resh-peh-yud-resh* (הרפיר); and

5. Longley, *lamed-nun-gimel-lamed-yud* (לנגלי).

Other prominent championship **five**-letter words include: *ketarim, kaf-tav-resh-yud-mem* (כתרים) crowns; as in *ḥamisha ketarim*, **five** (Bulls) NBA Crowns; and *rishon, resh-aleph-shin-vav-nun* (ראשון) first as in — "We're Number One!"

In a world filled with *maḥaloket* (conflict or controversy), one issue which remains beyond *maḥaloket*, is that the Chicago Bulls are the NBA Team of the '90s. The Chicago Bulls are Number One — **five** times!

Mazal Tov! Mazal Tov!! Mazal Tov!!! Mazal Tov!!!! Mazal Tov!!!!!

The Chicago Bulls
A Model of Family Harmony (*Shalom Bayit*)[8]

When the Chicago Bulls won their sixth NBA Championship, some questions remained. Was this indeed the "Last Dance" or would Phil Jackson, Michael Jordan, Scottie Pippen and Dennis Rodman sign contracts for a future "running of the Bulls," and how did the Bulls overcome such apparent discord to win the championship again this year?

The answer to the first question may be learned from the following story:

While holding a small bird in his hands, an anti-Semitic ruler in a medieval European Jewish community once approached a highly respected Rabbi.

> "Rabbi I am told that you are so wise that you are able to predict future events. If so, please tell me — will this bird live or die? If you are right this bird will live. If you are wrong, the bird will be killed."

The Rabbi responded:

> "I cannot tell you whether or not this innocent, frail bird will live or die. However, I can tell you that it's future lies entirely in your hands."

In a similar fashion, the future of the "Jordan Era" lay in the hands of Jerry Reinsdorf, Jerry Krause, Phil Jackson, Michael Jordan, Scottie Pippen and Dennis Rodman. Only these men could predict and control the immediate future of the Chicago Bulls.

The answer to the second question also is rooted deeply in spirituality. Although portrayed by many as a manifestation of discord, the post-'95 Chicago Bulls, in their own way, have been a sports model of the Jewish principle of *Shalom Bayit*.

Shalom Bayit, "peace (of the) home," refers to the sacred principle in Jewish tradition of maintaining tranquility in the home. A Jew is charged to do whatever it takes, within the parameters of Jewish law (*Halakha*), to maintain and enhance peaceful relationships. This principle promotes respectful, loving relationships between spouses, parents and children, siblings, and between grandparents and grandchildren.

This principle has been extended to include institutions beyond the private Jewish home such as Jewish-owned businesses, synagogues and other Jewish organizations.

Jewish tradition is replete with sources promoting *Shalom Bayit*.

The *Talmud* states:

> *Shalom (Bayit)* is so important that even the Holy One Blessed Be He made a change for its benefit [by altering Sara's unflattering words about Abraham when He reported them to him].
>
> (*Bava Metzia* 87a)

Maimonides in the *Mishneh Torah* provides a formula for *Shalom Bayit*:

> Our Sages commanded: a man should always eat less than his means, dress according to his means and show honor to his wife and children beyond his means.
>
> (Maimonides, *Mishneh Torah*, *Hilkhot Deiot* 5:10)

What are the prerequisites needed to achieve *Shalom Bayit*? They are the same as those that are needed to attain peace in general. In the *Torah*, we read of the three-fold Priestly blessing (*Birkat Kohanim*):

> *Y'varekh'kha Hashem v'yishm'rekha.*
> *Ya-er Hashem panav elekha vi-ḥuneka.*

Yisa Hashem panav elekha v'yasem l'kha shalom.

May the Lord bless you and watch over you.
May the Lord cause His face to shine upon you and be gracious to
you.
May the Lord lift his face upon you and bestow upon you peace.
                                                        (*Numbers* 6:24-26)

Ḥazal (Our Sages of Blessed Memory) teach that this series of blessings is stated in a progressive manner. The first blessing, comprised of only three (Hebrew) words, is for our material needs; that we be given the necessary material goods in order to sustain ourselves. The second blessing, comprised of five (Hebrew) words, is for our spiritual well-being; that we be illuminated with the light of the *Torah*. The third blessing, comprised of seven (Hebrew) words, is for the ultimate blessing of peace (*shalom*).

Shalom is related to the word *shalem* which means "whole" or "complete." In order to achieve a true (whole or complete) peace, we must have the peace of mind that our material and spiritual needs are adequately provided. Similarly, in order to attain and maintain *Shalom Bayit*, we must ensure the financial and spiritual stability of the Jewish household. Only then can we ensure tranquility. Not only is it important to live within a realistic financial budget agreed upon by both spouses, but husband and wife must be at one in terms of the religious philosophy of the household. To raise emotionally healthy children, both mother and father must share similar religious values and perspectives.

In Jewish history we look to Aaron, Moses' brother, as the role model for peace.

Rabbi Hillel says:

Be of the disciples of Aaron, loving peace and pursuing peace,
loving humankind and bringing them near to the *Torah*.
                                                (*Ethics of Our Fathers* 1:12)

We learn from Moses and the extreme professional demands placed upon him that, in order to maintain *Shalom Bayit*, family members must spend quality time with one another. In order to help alleviate some of his job-related stress, Jethro, Moses' father-in-law, devised a multi-tiered judicial system. After observing the over-demanding judicial schedule of Moses, Jethro exclaimed:

> This matter that you are doing is not good. You will surely wear yourself down along with this nation which is with you; because this matter is too heavy for you, you cannot manage it alone.
>
> (*Exodus* 18:17-18)

As a concerned father, father-in-law and grandfather, Jethro knew that the only way to create and then maintain *Shalom Bayit* in the household of Moses and his wife, Tzipora, was if the family spent more time together.

Shabbat, the Jewish Sabbath, is a day of extreme holiness. Not only do we dedicate this day to God, but to our families. It is a time for families to share festive meals, study together and attend synagogue. By achieving a closeness to each other, we become closer to God and help preserve and promote *Shalom Bayit*.

Noted author, Rabbi Hayim Halevy Donin of blessed memory, stresses that *Shalom Bayit* within the Jewish home is the key to *Shalom Bayit* within the Jewish community.

> The family is the core of Jewish society and a center of its religious life. If the home is strong in Jewish values, stable and healthy, then all of Jewish life and all its institutions — religious, educational, social etc. — will be alive and vibrant. And if the home is weak, emotionally, morally, and spiritually, all else will soon mirror that weakness.[9]

On June 14, 1998, the Chicago Bulls captured their sixth NBA Championship. Despite being weakened by age, injury and the public's intense focus on their future, the Bulls somehow managed to accomplish this awesome feat. Achieving their success was the way they established and maintained a sports version of *Shalom Bayit*.

Mainly to the credit of Coach Phil Jackson and team captain Michael Jordan, the Bulls consistently played a spirited team game made possible because of the participation of players and coaches who respected one another and were at relative peace with each other.

Over the last three years, the Bulls were confronted by numerous problems. Without proper team leadership, these problems could have caused irreparable dissension that would have destroyed the unity of the team. How did the Bulls maintain *Shalom Bayit?*

1. *The Michael Jordan Superstar Factor.*

   Under Jackson's tutelage, "MJ" evolved from a potentially self-centered superstar to a team player and leader. Not only is Jordan a superstar offensive player, but he is also a defensive one. His selfless, competitive spirit is contagious to his teammates. In particular, he helped inspire and raise the status of teammate Scottie Pippen from an "ordinary" NBA star to an elite NBA superstar.

2. *Phil Jackson: A Blend of the '60s and '90s.*

   Using discipline only when needed, Phil Jackson earned the utmost respect from his players and assistant coaches. He did this by applying his "laid-back, '60ish" approach to the players of the '90s. Most coaches probably would have great difficulty coaching Dennis Rodman because of his sometimes peculiar behavior. Jackson, however, bonded with Rodman and reinforced his many positive qualities, while downplaying his off-court antics. He also persuaded his other players to adopt the tolerant philosophy that "Dennis is Dennis" and, as long as he plays his hardest for the team, his off-court diversions should be ignored. Because of Jackson's patience and tolerance, Rodman's on-court behavior and play was at its best this past year.

3. *Would Jackson, Jordan, Pippen and/or Rodman Return?*

   While almost taking for granted that the Bulls would win a sixth championship, the media focused on whether Jackson, Jordan, Pippen and Rodman would rejoin the Bulls next year. Despite this repeated distraction throughout the season, Jackson was able to inspire his players to focus on each game.

Although it was Bulls Vice President Jerry Krause who hired Jackson and gave him his first opportunity to coach in the NBA, it is no secret that the two are no longer friends. In a recent *New York Times* article, Ira Berkow writes:

> It is true that Jackson and Krause — the man who hired him — no longer have any love lost for each other. "I'm not really sure what the problem is, but I think Krause thinks I've gotten a big head," Jackson said. Krause won't comment on the acrimonious relationship other than to say, "I'm going to take the high road — there's no traffic up there."[10]

Despite this additional distraction, Jackson did not allow his battle with management to interfere with the Bulls play.

In a similar manner, Jackson kept other management-team feuds from affecting the team. For a number of years, Scottie Pippen made it known to the public that he was upset he was receiving a relatively low salary for a player of his talent in the NBA. In response, the team's management made it very clear to the public that, in 1991, Pippen himself chose to sign a long-term contract with the Bulls risking this very predicament. Taking a lesson of *Shalom Bayit* from Jackson, Pippen did not allow his contractual displeasure to affect his on-court contribution.

Shalom Bayit is built upon love and respect. In order for peace and tranquility to exist in the Jewish home, husband and wife must be at one with each other. Similarly, the children must manifest their love and respect for their parents, siblings and grandparents.

Perhaps the greatest illustration of love, respect and devotion to one's family was that displayed by Ruth the Moabite for her mother-in-law Naomi. After Ruth's husband, brother-in-law and father-in-law all died prematurely in Moab, Ruth — despite Naomi's Herculean efforts to the contrary — decided to accompany Naomi back to Israel:

> ...Do not plead with me to leave you to return after following you; for wherever you go I will go, wherever you lodge I will lodge; your

nation is my nation and your God is my God. Wherever you die I
will die and there will I be buried; thus the Lord will do to me and
thus may He do more, because only death will separate me from
you.

(*Ruth* 1:16-17)

Michael Jordan, in an example of the love and respect the Bulls players have for
their beloved coach, repeatedly stated that his future with the Bulls depended,
in large part, on Phil Jackson's future. Had MJ made his declaration in "Ruth-
like" terms, he most likely would have said something like, "Wherever Coach
Jackson goes, I'll go. If Phil returns to coach the Bulls, I'll return to play for the
Bulls. Only retirement or the coach's blessings will separate me from my
beloved coach."

This is the essence of *Shalom Bayit*. No wonder the Bulls are six time
champions![11]

May You Go from Strength to Strength

What do Michael Jordan, Jerry Seinfeld and Moses all have in common? No, Michael is *not* Jewish.

All three of these world-renowned figures achieved greatness in their given fields and left while still on the top. After nine successful years as one of television's top shows, NBC announced that the 1997-1998 season would be *Seinfeld's* last. After about forty years, serving as leader of the Israelites, Moses — arguably Israel's all-time best leader — was commanded by God to "retire" from his post. Although 120 years old at the time, Moses — a True Hero[12] — was still functioning at a top level. In fact, the *Torah* describes Moses at that time, "his eye had not dimmed and his strength had not escaped" *(Deuteronomy 34:7)*.

On January 7, 1999, NBA basketball fans rejoiced when it was announced that a resolution had been reached between the owners and the Players Union, thus ending the NBA lockout. Although there would be an abbreviated regular season, there still would be a season. The next burning question was — would Michael Jordan return? This was of great concern not only to the Chicago Bulls management and fans, but to the NBA and its millions of fans. After all, Michael Jordan was desperately needed to help attract fans back to NBA games, especially since many resented the lockout.

On January 13, Michael Jordan formally announced his retirement from the Chicago Bulls and the NBA. Even though he completed the 1997-1998 season as the NBA's Most Valuable Player, he decided that now was the time to leave. Like Jerry Seinfeld, he made this decision while at the height of his success, on his own terms. Like Seinfeld, Michael Jordan made this decision despite great public pressure to stay on.

In discussing his upcoming "retirement," Jerry Seinfeld stressed the importance of leaving while at the top of his profession. In Seinfeld's own words, "I felt...the Moment. That's the only way I can describe it... If I get off now I have a chance at a standing ovation. That's what you go for."[13]

Although Jordan's retirement may be an emotional shock, it surely comes as no surprise. After all, for some time, Michael Jordan has spoken of the importance of leaving while at the top of his game. How much more on top could one become? In addition to being the NBA's greatest star, Jordan made the winning basket that brought the Bulls their sixth championship and was appropriately rewarded as the MVP of the NBA Playoff Finals. At the retirement press conference, Michael Jordan reiterated the importance of retiring from basketball while at the top of his game:

> ...I chose to walk away knowing I could still play the game. That's what I always wished for... That's exactly the way I wanted to end it.[14]

Even though Michael Jordan could have continued to play and thrill millions of fans for at least one more season, I feel that he made the right decision. He left on his own terms at the pinnacle of his career. Unfortunately, too many star athletes decide to continue playing although their skills are diminished. Many of us remember watching the final stages of the careers of two of baseball's greatest players, Willie Mays and Hank Aaron. Although it was nostalgic to watch Mays and Aaron play for teams fielded by the cities where they began their Major League careers, it hurt to watch these great athletes perform at a level far below their primes. Unfortunately, these two great stars, along with many others, decided to retire too late. Michael Jordan, however, did not make this same mistake. Jordan, like Moses, retired while he physically could perform at his professional peak.

Also like *Moshe Rabbenu* (Moses Our Teacher), when Michael retired, he was regarded as the best ever in his occupation. As the *Torah* teaches: "And another prophet has not arisen in Israel like Moses" (*Deuteronomy 34:10*). In the world of basketball similar accolades have been stated regarding MJ. In fact, the inscription on the monument sculpted in Jordan's honor reads:

"the greatest there ever was,
the greatest there ever will be"

In Jewish tradition there is a concept known as *hakarat ha-tov*. It means "recognizing the good." It refers to acknowledging a job well done, by giving credit where credit is due.

After Michael Jordan announced his retirement, the first to give thanks to MJ were two prominent Jewish sports figures — Chicago Bulls Chairman Jerry Reinsdorf and NBA Commissioner David Stern.

In that spirit it is most fitting to extend our appreciation to MJ. It did not take long to realize how lucky we were to witness the performance of such a great athlete as Michael Jordan. Thank you, Michael, for providing us, your countless fans, with the opportunity to enjoy your play. Thank you for your dedicated style of team play and competitiveness which inspired our lives. As you now enter your full-time life off the court, may you be blessed with similar challenges, successes and peace of mind as you were during your basketball career. May you continue to go from strength to strength.

Stars, Stripes and *Magen Davids* Forever

At the very beginning of *The Book of Leviticus,* the *Torah* teaches:

> And He called out to Moses and the Lord spoke to him from the Tent of Meeting saying: "Speak to the Children of Israel and say to them, when a man from among you makes a sacrifice to the Lord…"
>
> (*Leviticus* 1:1-2)

Many everlasting Jewish lessons can be learned from these two opening verses.

Lesson #1: Humility

We learn from *Moshe Rabbenu* (Moses our Teacher) to be humble in life. Our Sages teach us that the reason the Hebrew letter *aleph* of the word *Va-Yikra* (ויקרא) "and He called out" is written in a miniature fashion in the *Torah* is to stress how modest Moses was. Even though God called out to him, Moses remained a most humble man (*anav*).[15] As Jews, no matter how accomplished we may be, we must always remember that "humility is the best policy."

Lesson #2: Visibility

We are a very visible people. The miniature *aleph* in the word *Va-Yikra* also reminds us that as a people, our actions are being watched by the rest of the world. We must be careful that our actions reflect our high moral standards.

Lesson #3: Closeness to God

We must always bring ourselves closer to God. One of the most often used words in Leviticus is "*Korban*." *Korban* is usually translated as an offering or a sacrifice. Actually, *korban* comes from the Hebrew word *karov* which means *close*. During the days of the Tabernacle (*Mishkan*) and in later Temple days, the primary way in which a Jew brought himself closer to God was by bringing a *korban*. Since the destruction of the Second Temple, prayer has replaced sacrifices as the primary method of bringing ourselves closer to God.

Lesson #4: Making Sacrifices

As Jews, we must always make sacrifices. In Yiddish, there is an old saying, "*iz shver tzu zayn a Yid,*" or "it is tough being a Jew." In order to lead a committed Jewish life in the Diaspora, inevitably we must make certain lifestyle changes. For example, a *Shomer Shabbat* (Sabbath-observant Jew) sometimes must work on Sundays since working on Saturdays is in violation of the Sabbath.

I was reminded of these four Jewish "Leviticus Life Lessons" by a 1996 news item receiving a lot of media coverage. This story appeared on the front page in the sports sections of American newspapers, as well as in the religion columns of our nation's papers.

This story concerns Chris Jackson. Jackson at that time was an NBA Denver Nugget star better known by his Muslim name, Mahmoud Abdul-Rauf.[16] For about four months, Abdul-Rauf decided not to stand in accordance with NBA standards when the National Anthem was played prior to each Nugget basketball game.

According to Abdul-Rauf, the Star Spangled Banner is a "symbol of oppression and tyranny."[17] Abdul-Rauf stated further, "[My] beliefs are more important... My duty is to my creator, not to nationalistic ideology..."[18]

The NBA finally reacted by suspending Abdul-Rauf. Later, his suspension was lifted when Abdul-Rauf agreed to stand during the National Anthem.

As a proud American Jew who supports the First Amendment and its promotion of the free exercise of religion, I was very troubled by this incident. I respect Abdul-Rauf for taking a position in the name of religion, but I am deeply disturbed by his behavior. His actions are contrary to the four lessons outlined earlier.

Lesson #1: Humility

Abdul-Rauf's behavior was self-centered and drew a lot of public attention. Also, it is hypocritical of a man to accept $2.6 million a year for shooting a ball through a hoop, and at the same time accuse this country of being tyrannical and oppressive.

Lesson #2: Visibility

As Jews living in a "foreign" land, we live with the reality that Jews and Muslims are both minorities in America. Minorities are constantly in the public eye and scrutinized. Furthermore, as Jews, we are guided by the principle first introduced by the *Talmudic* Sage Samuel known as "*dina d'malkhuta dina,*" or "the law of the kingdom is the law" *(Bava Kamma* 113a). This principle reinforces the lesson that, with few exceptions, we must abide by the laws of our host country. Unfortunately, instead of bringing honor to his religion, Abdul-Rauf's behavior brought shame to his Islamic faith.

Lesson #3: Closeness to God

I respect Abdul-Rauf for wanting to be closer to his god, but there are other ways to achieve this spiritual goal.

Lesson #4: Making Sacrifices

In American Labor Law, there is a policy known as "reasonable accommodation." By law, an employer is required to make reasonable accommodations for employees regarding potential restrictive issues like religion. However, it might be considered an *unreasonable* accommodation for the NBA to relax its Anthem stand-up rule for a player who agreed to abide by this rule when he signed his most recent contract. Also, it is not clear whether the NBA's position infringes upon the free exercise of Abdul-Rauf's religion. There are times in life when we must make certain sacrifices. By agreeing to stand up during the Anthem and pray, Abdul-Rauf indeed made a sacrifice.

As Jews with a holy tradition, we must use this unfortunate episode as a reminder that we can live as observant, committed Jews in a secular American society, promoting *Stars, Stripes and Magen Davids Forever*. In order to do so, however, there are times when we must make certain minimal sacrifices which ultimately bring us closer to God. It is important to be humble and to remember that we are a very visible people. Ultimately, when we behave in a respectful manner towards others without compromising our own belief system, we become even closer to God.

Good As I Should Be
Dennis Rodman and Jewish Tradition

People look for role models in life, people to emulate, those to shape their behaviors, those to look up to. According to Jewish tradition, Jews are directed to seek out such role models as our parents, grandparents, teachers, Rabbis and great figures in Jewish history. We do so by incorporating their ethical character traits (*midot*) into our everyday lives.

Unfortunately, our youth in America too frequently look for heroes and role models in the wrong places. They mistakenly admire people who may be most talented professionally, but who lead wretched personal lives. Individuals who are particularly prone to being considered as role models by our youth include movie stars and sports figures.

Some sports stars probably warrant emulation and could be referred to as "Limited Sports Heroes." Many Limited Sports Heroes regularly engage in exemplary off-field behavior and activities such as acts of charity. Other players, who aside from their illustrious on-field performance, lead lifestyles *contrary* to those we would wish for our children. These athletes serve as examples of **how not to be**.

Dennis Rodman, one of the greatest defensive players in the history of the National Basketball Association, is one of these examples of how *not* to be.[19]

Appropriately, Dennis Rodman called his 1996 autobiography, *Bad As I Wanna Be*. In his mind, perhaps, being a "free spirit" entitles one to be "bad as you wanna be."

The traditional Jewish formula of being a free spirit, however, prohibits an individual from being "bad as he may wanna be." One must live within certain boundaries, the boundaries prescribed by the *Torah* and the laws of the land. Instead of promoting the philosophy of "bad as I wanna be," being a free spirit in Jewish tradition promotes being "good as I should be!"

A prime example of how **"not to be,"** is Rodman's desecration of his body with his many tattoos, and the numerous rings which pierce unconventional parts of his anatomy.

In this respect we are commanded in the *Torah*:

> And you shall not make an incision in your flesh for the dead nor shall you tattoo yourselves; I am the Lord.
>
> (*Leviticus* 19:28)

The *Torah* also addresses the prohibition against dressing in clothes worn by the opposite sex, another reason not to emulate Rodman.

> A man's garments shall not be worn by a woman, and neither shall a man wear a woman's garment; for it is an abomination of the Lord for anyone who does this.
>
> (*Deuteronomy* 22:5)

Head butting a referee, pushing players with excessive force, using inappropriate language in media interviews, and the lack of proper honor (*kavod*) and respect (*derekh eretz*) are all Rodman characteristics. For Jews, this is a lesson in the saying, *"derekh eretz kadma la-Torah,"* "Proper respect precedes *even* the study of *Torah*."

A highly visible American Jew who has been involved throughout Rodman's career has been David Stern, the Commissioner of the NBA. The Commissioner's role is to act in the "best interests" of the game at all times, even though his interpretation may not always be in agreement with the interpretation of all of his employers, the team owners. From David Stern's actions we have learned more about another important Jewish tradition — meting out punishment commensurate with the crime committed.

During a game played in Minnesota against the Timberwolves in January of

1997, after battling for a rebound, Dennis Rodman, then a Chicago Bull, kicked a courtside cameraman.[20]

Stern initially punished Dennis Rodman by suspending him without pay for at least 11 games. Financially, this suspension cost Rodman in excess of one million dollars. He was required to go through mandatory counseling sessions. This latter requirement apparently was dropped, probably because the Commissioner became convinced that the NBA legally did not have the appropriate authority.[21] At the end of the 11 game suspension, Stern made it clear to Rodman that if he did not control his behavior, he risked being banned from ever again playing in the NBA:

> I am satisfied that Dennis recognizes that his conduct in the Minnesota game was unacceptable. Dennis told me that while he does not plan to change the way he plays the game, he will conform his conduct on the playing court to acceptable standards. And he knows that any further incidents of this nature may end his career in the NBA.
> — Commissioner David Stern, commenting on the incident.[22]

In Jewish tradition, the ideal punishment is one in which the injured party is justly compensated, and where the world learns that such behavior is unacceptable (punitive). The ideal punishment is also one in which the perpetrator of the wrong learns from the mistakes, and is truly sorry for his actions. Such responses are known as *teshuva* (repentance or return).

The punishment ordered by Commissioner Stern was designed for Rodman to achieve the secular equivalent of *teshuva*. Ideally, Dennis Rodman would "rebound" from his punishment, realize that what he did was wrong, apologize to those he wronged and, feeling remorse for his actions, would resolve not to commit such acts ever again.

From the public's perception, perhaps Dennis Rodman achieved all of these components of *teshuva*.

When Rodman finally apologized to the camerman, he essentially apologized to his teammates and to the Bulls management. His public statements seemed to point towards a feeling of remorse and a resolution not to repeat his errors.

It may be argued that Rodman even achieved what Maimonides describes as perfect repentance (*teshuva g'mura*):

> What is considered perfect repentance? When a person is confronted with the same circumstances that existed when he sinned in the past, and he has the opportunity to repeat the sin, but this time he resists because of his desire to repent...
>
> (Maimonides, *Mishneh Torah, Hilkhot Teshuva* 2:1)

As I recall, in Rodman's first game back after his suspension, as he aggressively chased a loose ball, Rodman again ran into a cameraman at the United Center. This time, however, instead of kicking the cameraman, he gave him a gentle tap on the chest. Perhaps this is what Maimonides meant by perfect repentance!

I am not sure whether Rodman truly feels remorse for his actions or whether he can realistically control himself from similar future outbursts.

Dennis Rodman in many ways participated in an act of *teshuva* by pledging his first 11 games salary after his return from the suspension to numerous charities. Although this one charitable act is deserving of emulation, Dennis Rodman is still not my hero, not even a Limited Sports Hero.

In Jewish life and in society as well, it is not right to be as "bad as I wanna be," rather, we should all strive to be as "good as I should be."

CHAPTER 3

FOOTBALL
A Season for Breaking and Building

"…a season to break and a season to build."
(*Ecclesiastes* 3:3)

Perhaps the sport which best exemplifies this verse from *Ecclesiastes*, is football. "The best offense is a good defense." Defenses break the opponent down and offenses build the team up.

The Value of a Positive (Sports) Self-Image

Our Sages taught that the adult generation of the Children of Israel who left Egypt was not allowed to enter the Land of Israel because of its involvement in the episode of the Golden Calf and by supporting the evil report issued by the Ten Spies.

The *Torah* teaches (*Numbers* 13:2) that each spy was a leader from one of the twelve tribes of Israel. When the spies returned from checking out the Land, two reports were issued. One was the joint report of Joshua and Caleb, and the second report was issued collectively by the remaining ten spies. Although both reports were truthful, they were much different from each other. Additionally, the authors of the two reports received totally opposite responses from God. For their report, Joshua and Caleb received the ultimate reward of being allowed to enter Israel. On the other hand, the report of the Ten Spies provoked a negative response from the Almighty.

If both reports were truthful, then why was the reaction of God so diverse? The Ten Spies reported that the Land of Israel was a beautiful land, but major obstacles which would prevent the Israelites from conquering it existed.

The Ten Spies lacked confidence in their own ability to overcome such obstacles and they lacked faith that God would assist them in meeting such challenges. These ten leaders of Israel had a very poor self-image:

> And there we saw the *Nephilim* the sons of giants from the *Nephilim*; and we were in our own eyes like grasshoppers and so were we in their eyes.
>
> (*Numbers* 13:33)

Not only did the Ten Spies feel insignificant, but they also were convinced that the *Nephilim* thought of them as being worthless.

In spite of being greatly physically outmatched, Joshua and Caleb nevertheless showed their leadership, their belief in God and evidence of a positive self-image when they insisted that the Children of Israel would indeed conquer the Land of Israel.

What ultimately separated Joshua and Caleb from the other ten spies was that they not only possessed a superior level of faith in the Almighty, but they also had a positive self-image.

In life, positive self-image is a key to success. Often times, this separates the leaders from the followers and the winners from the losers.

Participating in sports is a major contributor to self-image. Not only does the physical activity make a person feel healthy, but there always seems to be a sport in which each individual can either excel, or at least feel good about themselves. Some people prefer individual sports like tennis or golf over team sports such as baseball, football or basketball. Still others prefer to participate in sports like soccer where there is limited attention on the individual player.

I believe that being involved in sports is important in shaping the self-image of a team's fans as well as its host city or university. The moods of sports fans may be impacted daily by the success of their teams.

While a student at the University of Michigan, I found the social atmosphere of fall Saturday nights to be dictated by how the Michigan Wolverines fared on the gridiron earlier that day. If they won, Saturday night was a time of festivity. If they lost, a most rare occasion, the mood on campus was somber, and if they beat their 1970s archival — Ohio State — the campus was out of control!

Chicago, for many years, was a city with a poor sports self-image. It was a city resigned to losing. After all, the Cubs have been out of the World Series since 1948, the White Sox last played in the World Series in 1959 and the Black Hawks last won the Stanley Cup in 1961. Aside from a few strong years from the DePaul Blue Demon basketball team, Chicago sports teams consistently cast a pall of gloom and defeat.

In the mid-1980s and 1990s, the stars of the financial world — the Bulls and Bears, suddenly became the stars of the world of Chicago sports. The Bears captured their first-ever Super Bowl victory following the 1985 season and the

Bulls won their first-ever NBA Championship five years later. Chicago was able to shed its "wait until next year, Charlie Brown" losing attitude and "The City of Big Shoulders" was indeed a city with big sports shoulders. Chicagoans finally began to develop a positive sports self-image.

Led by Coach Mike Ditka, the 1985 Chicago Bears was perhaps one of the most colorful sports teams of all times. Like Joshua and Caleb, Ditka instilled the importance of a positive self-image in his players. Never devoid of controversy, the team was led by Jim McMahon, the "Punky Q. B.," who played more like a lineman than a quarterback. McMahon was joined in the backfield by the best all-time running back in NFL history, Walter Payton. In a display of the ultimate in positive self-image, Ditka would, on certain plays from scrimmage, let McMahon hand the ball off to William "The Fridge" Perry, in a draw play from the backfield. Through the coaching leadership of Mike Ditka and his defensive coordinator Buddy Ryan, the 1985 Chicago Bears emerged once again as "The Monsters of the Midway."

Following the Bears overwhelming defeat of the New England Patriots in the 1986 Super Bowl in New Orleans, the Bears were welcomed back in below- zero weather by thousands of fans who lined the streets of downtown Chicago to toast their parading champs.

Unfortunately, the City of Chicago did not repeat this euphoria until the 1990-1991 basketball season. In that year another "Joshua-like" leader transformed a franchise that had failed to win a championship.

Michael Jordan, the best player to ever grace the hardwood floor, had proven himself a true team player. Much like his contemporaries, Magic Johnson and Larry Bird, Michael Jordan became a team leader. His extraordinary level of play helped inspire his teammates to attain higher levels of basketball ability. Under the tutelage of Coach Phil Jackson and Jordan, the rest of the Bulls players began to believe that they could overcome all opposing teams. They were no longer like the grasshoppers, but were the giants!

When the Bulls reached the NBA playoff finals in 1991, many Bulls fans questioned their team's ability to "enter the promised land" by defeating the "giants" of the NBA — the L.A. Lakers.

However, under the inspired leadership of Coach Jackson and Michael Jordan, the Bulls adopted the same attitude promoted by Joshua and Caleb.

They became "giants" and transformed Magic Johnson and the Lakers from Los Angeles into "grasshoppers."

Once again, the City of Chicago reveled in its positive sports self-image. Not only were the Bulls champions, but so were their fans.

The rest is history. From this point on, Chicago sports fans expected success. No longer did they walk around with long faces and droopy shoulders, mumbling, "Wait until next year!" The Bulls and Bears instilled a feeling of "Yes we can! We can win!" This was a positive (sports) self-image that many, perhaps, took with them to work, to their homes and to their synagogues.

As Jews, we too must always carry with us a positive self-image, a self-image that will motivate us to attain even greater levels of spiritual success. We need to maintain a self-image that will inspire us to overcome the problems which face our people, a self-image that will inspire us to further develop our Jewish communities and institutions, and a self-image which will inspire us so that we remain a vibrant people with a safe and secure religious homeland — Israel. We need to always maintain a self-image that will make us feel like "giants" and not "grasshoppers!"

Maccabees, Miracles and Wildcats

Our Sages teach:

> "We should not depend on miracles."
>
> *("Ein somkhin ahl ha-nes.")*

Our modern day pundits teach:

> "God helps those who help themselves."

These two statements summarize the basic principles of miracles in Jewish theology. On the one hand, we know that if we do our jobs, God will do His. In this sense, miracles do indeed occur. On the other hand, we cannot lead our lives depending on miracles.

There is an old joke about a flooded town being evacuated by the local authorities. When the rescuers came by car to Abe Goldberg's house and offered him a ride, Goldberg refused, claiming, "God will provide."

The waters continued to rise and, an hour later, rescuers came in a boat and offered Abe a ride. Goldberg refused again insisting that, "God will take care of me."

Finally, Goldberg's house was submerged and the rescuers came in a helicopter and found Abe standing on the roof. The rescuers threw a rope to Goldberg and pleaded with him to grab it. With his neck barely above the water, Goldberg refused to take the rope, once again insisting, "God will provide. The Almighty will save me!"

After drowning, Goldberg appears before the Heavenly Court and complains to the Almighty:

> "Master of the Universe, I believed in You during my entire life. Why did You fail to save me?"

God responded:

> "Abe, what are you *kvetching* about? First I sent you a car, then a boat and finally a helicopter!"

On *Ḥanukah* we recall and celebrate two main miracles: the miracle of the Temple oil and, the miracle of the military conquest.

The *Talmud* (*Shabbat* 21b) discusses the miracle of the oil. When the Maccabean armies conquered Jerusalem they entered the Holy Temple and cleansed it both physically and spiritually. They then searched for *kosher*, uncontaminated oil in order to re-light the *Menorah*. The search turned up only one, single pitcher of *kosher* oil capable of lighting all eight branches of the *Menorah* for only one 24-hour day. However, instead of burning for only one day, a miracle occurred and this same quantity of oil burned for eight days.

Our Sages teach that each day, the *Kohanim* (priests) would take the oil from the single pitcher, divide it into eight equal portions and place a quantity of oil enough for three hours in the *Menorah*. Each day, God would ensure that the oil burned for an additional 21 hours. The *Kohanim*, in effect, were partners in this miracle.[1]

The second miracle also involved a partnership between God and the Maccabean-led Jewish armed forces. Greatly outnumbered by the evil Antiokhus Epiphanes and his armies, our ancestors overcame overwhelming odds and defeated the Assyrian-Greeks. Along with their military victory came the spiritual victory of reinstating the freedom to study *Torah* and practice Judaism.[2]

Rabbi Ben-Tzion Firer in his book *Eleh Hem Moadai*, discusses the necessary interplay between the human and Divine roles in order to bring about a miracle. For a Divine miracle on the magnitude of the *Ḥanukah* miracles to occur, the ultimate beneficiary must first have the courage to take the required leap of faith. Such leaps of faith were taken by *Naḥshon ben Aminadav* when he jumped into the unsettling waters of the Red Sea and Mattathias and his sons as they challenged the far more numerous and powerful Assyrian-Greek armies.[3]

When we recite the *Ahl ha-Nissim* prayer on Ḥanukah, we recall the miracle of God's special role in the military victory. This prayer is recited in the Grace After Meals (*Birkat ha-Mazon*) and *Amidah* prayer:

> (We thank You) for the miracles, (and) for the redemption, (and) for the mighty deeds, (and) for the rescues and for the wars, that You performed for our fathers in those days at this season.

Even though we do not rely on miracles, we must always remember that if not for God's help, none of our "battle plans" will come to pass. We learn from the miracles of Ḥanukah that all we must do is open the door of life just a little bit and God will open it up the rest of the way.

As a child, I used to include prayers for my favorite sports teams in my *davening*. As an adult, I act in a more appropriate manner and I now keep my prayers out of the sports arena.[4] If an underdog team overcomes overwhelming odds and wins a game or an event, I refuse to deem it a Divine miracle. I prefer instead to call it a "Sports Miracle."

The three greatest Sports Miracles I have witnessed were the world championships of the 1969 New York Mets and the 1969 New York Jets, along with the winning of the gold medal by the 1980 U.S. Olympic hockey team.

Not only were the '69 Mets nicknamed the "Amazing Mets," but they were also known as the "Miracle Mets." They received this nickname for their team's "miraculous" rally in defeating the Chicago Cubs, the Atlanta Braves and, finally, the Baltimore Orioles in the World Series.

Projected as major underdogs in their 1969 Super Bowl match with the Baltimore Colts, the New York Jets — led by a young, brash quarterback named Joe Namath — performed a Sports Miracle and upset the Colts 16-7.

In the 1980 Winter Olympics, a less talented but highly motivated amateur ice hockey team overcame great odds, defeating the highly skilled U.S.S.R. squad 4-3. By winning the Olympic gold medal, these dedicated American athletes achieved what the media dubbed as "The Miracle on Ice;" these spirited hockey players participated in a Sports Miracle.

From a Jewish theological perspective, Sports Miracles are not in the same "league" or "ballpark" as are Divine miracles, but the concept of "team play" is the same. A team or group must work together in order to expect Divine intervention; or in the case of a Sports Miracle — a little luck.

In 1995, more than 25 years after "Broadway Joe" Namath "guaranteed" a Jet victory in Super Bowl III, I witnessed the greatest Sports Miracle in my lifetime. That miracle was the championship of the Northwestern Wildcat football team. By winning the Big Ten title, the Wildcats attained something that had not been achieved in 59 years. They also earned the right to play in the revered New Year's Day Rose Bowl game, an honor they had not earned since 1949.

When former Wildcat coach Gary Barnett came to Northwestern, he inspired his players to believe in themselves even though the school had accepted losing as a part of its tradition.[5] Rather than expecting either to lose or receive a miracle, Gary Barnett taught his student-athletes to "Expect Victory!"[6]

In this same fashion, it was Mattathias, Judah the Maccabee's father, who first rallied the Jewish troops together, inspiring them to believe in God, in the *Torah* and in themselves. Hellenism was not the way to go, even though many contemporary Jews at that time chose to assimilate.

The purpose of the war that Judah the Maccabee and his soldiers fought was to achieve a most holy mission, one to reinstate the free practice of *Torah* Judaism.

In order for Judah to bring God to his side, he had to first convince the Almighty of the cohesiveness and dedication of his supporters. In that respect, the Maccabean army fought a most spirited "team war."

Similarly, in order for Northwestern to become a champion and defeat such football powerhouses as Notre Dame, Penn State and Michigan, they had to play flawless dedicated, team football. This was indeed a Sports Miracle!

Unlike Sports Miracles, not every Divine miracle is open and obvious like the splitting of the Red Sea, the Revelation at Mount Sinai or Israel's victory in the Six Day War. Most of God's miracles are hidden. Each time a healthy baby is born, it is a Divine miracle. Each day when one wakes up healthy, it is a Divine miracle. In fact, we thank God each day for this miracle by reciting the appropriate prayers. Sadly, on too many occasions, people overlook these everyday Divine miracles and take them for granted.

The best way to bring about Divine miracles is to believe in God and in His power to perform miracles, but not to depend on them. If we do our part in life, God will do His. By following this path, when we least expect it, miracles will occur.

CHAPTER 4

HOCKEY

A Season for Crying and Laughing

"A season to cry and a season to laugh…"
(*Ecclesiastes* 3:4)

I *once went to a boxing match and a hockey game broke out.* Hockey, as this one-liner connotes, can be — at times — a most violent sport. Many times it is also a sport in which the players engage in great on-ice celebrations. For example, when a player scores three goals in one game, even the fans join in the celebration by tossing hats onto the ice rink, acknowledging the "hat trick." Perhaps more than any other sport, hockey is a game in which extreme emotions are constantly exhibited.

Just Do It! Bo Knows Free Will & Courage and So Do Mario & Jim

From the late-1980s to the mid-1990s, the nickname "Bo" became a sports household word. This was Bo as in "Bo Knows" and as in **Bo Jackson**. What made Bo so appealing to sports fans was his hard work and desire to succeed as a two-sport athlete. During the summer he played baseball and during the fall he engaged in, what he referred to as his "hobby," professional football. Bo Jackson maximized his **freedom of choice** in deciding that he wanted to compete and excel in two sports. He lived the motto of the shoes which he endorsed — he "just *did* it!"

Ironically, one of the main lessons taught in the *Torah* portion (*parasha*), which is also named *Bo* (*Exodus* 10:1 — 13:16), is the importance of exercising free will/freedom of choice and to "just do it!" In Hebrew, this concept is known as *b'ḥira ḥofshit*.

Parashat Bo includes the final three of the Ten Plagues: locusts, darkness, and the killing of the first born. In light of the fact that the Almighty is merciful even to our enemies, the question exists: Why did God decree ten plagues? Why didn't He bring about just one plague which would have freed the Israelites and, in so doing, cause relatively minimal destruction? In the words of *Parashat Bo* and paraphrasing Nike, why didn't God "just do it!"?

One answer provided by our Sages is that God wanted to create an irrefutable record of His power for eternity. Ten plagues, along with the miraculous splitting of the Red Sea, have a far greater impact than does one single plague. A second possible answer is that by bringing about multiple plagues, God was better able to teach the world the importance of *b'ḥira ḥofshit*.

Ultimately, the Almighty wanted Pharaoh and the Egyptians to reach — on their own — the correct and just conclusion of providing the Israelites their freedom. Unfortunately, despite numerous opportunities, Pharaoh refused to free the Israelite slaves.

Jewish tradition promotes both freedom of choice/free will and predestination. Although these two complex philosophical concepts appear to be mutually exclusive, they can be reconciled and can even co-exist and augment each other. In this regard, Rabbi Akiva stated: "All is foreseen [by God], yet freedom [of choice] is given [to humankind]" (*Ethics of Our Fathers* 3:19). Even though certain matters in life may indeed be predestined, we must live our lives as if nothing is predestined.[1]

I once had a high school teacher who did not use the seat belt in his car. When confronted by his caring students, his response was, "When the good Lord decides that my time has arrived, a seat belt won't help!" This contradicts traditional Jewish thought. Jewish tradition teaches us *always* to buckle up! God helps those who help themselves!

Throughout our daily lives we make both simple and complex choices. When confronted by life's challenges, we choose how to meet these challenges.

Perhaps the most inspiring lessons of "just do it" may be learned from people who suffer medical adversity. Hockey's "Super Mario" Lemieux, baseball's Jim Abbott, and Bo Jackson each were confronted with severe physical handicaps, but chose to work their hardest to overcome these great obstacles. Instead of giving up, they chose to "just do it!"

In 1991, Jackson severely fractured his left hip while playing football for the National Football League's Los Angeles Raiders. This severe injury forced Bo to retire from football, and he was advised to retire from baseball as well. Accordingly, the Kansas City Royals cut him from their roster. However, Bo Jackson refused to give up his professional sports career, and signed with the Chicago White Sox. After extensive rehabilitation in 1991 and a subsequent hip replacement surgery, Bo returned to baseball despite his physical limitations. Through his hard work and great desire to succeed, Bo proved to himself and to the world that he *could* just do it!

Mario Lemieux is one of the greatest hockey players to have ever played the game. He spent his entire career with the Pittsburgh Penguins and helped them win the Stanley Cup several times. On a number of occasions, Lemieux also has won the National Hockey League scoring title and has appropriately earned the nickname "Super Mario."

Perhaps Mario's most "super" achievement occurred in 1992 when he was diagnosed with Hodgkin's disease. This form of cancer not only threatened his career as a hockey player, but his life as well. Rather than retire from professional hockey, Lemieux instead chose to play and fight the disease. He made the choice to "just do it!"

"Anytime you have an injury like this you have to have courage. But I didn't have any choice. It's in my nature to fight back," said Lemieux.[2]

After sitting out for about a month while undergoing intensive radiation treatments, Super Mario returned to the Penguin line-up and, in his first game back, scored a goal and an assist. Although he missed 23 games that season, Lemieux still won his fourth NHL scoring title. When he retired in November of 1997, the Hockey Hall of Fame chose to waive its mandatory waiting period and inducted the star player into its prestigious society.

Perhaps the most inspirational lesson in the annals of sports history is the story of Jim Abbott. Born without a right hand, Abbott, with the support of his family, refused to live the life of a handicapped person. Not only was he successful in his daily life but, through his dedication and hard work, Abbott excelled in sports. Jim Abbott maximized his freedom of choice. He chose not to be one who would seek compassion from others, but rather, became a person who would inspire others through his actions.

As a young child, Jim's father taught him how to play baseball and successfully use a mitt, despite his handicap. Jim Abbott worked so hard that he became a star pitcher in high school and also the varsity's starting quarterback! In 1987, as a baseball player at the University of Michigan, Abbott was named the amateur baseball player of the year and in 1988, as a star on the U.S. Olympic baseball team, Abbott was awarded the prestigious Sullivan Award as the nation's top amateur athlete.

After his collegiate career, Jim Abbott played Major League Baseball for the California Angels, New York Yankees, Chicago White Sox and Milwaukee Brewers. A highlight of his Major League career was pitching a no-hitter for the

Yankees in 1993. Former Angels pitching coach Marcel Lachemann was right when he stated, "We'll never see another like him."[3]

In our lives, we each have the choice to directly face our challenges and try to overcome them or to give up. Throughout our history as a nation, we Jews repeatedly have been challenged to give up our faith. However, because of the dedication of so many "Bo's" in each generation, many of whom died *ahl Kiddush Hashem* — while sanctifying God's Holy name, *K'lal Yisrael* (the World Jewish Community) remains strong. Ultimately, we remain a people with both a heritage and a land because of all those who "just do it!"

CHAPTER 5

GOLF

A Season for Scattering and Gathering Stones

"A season to cast stones and a season to gather stones..."
(*Ecclesiastes* 3:5)

Pebble Beach, host of the prestigious Professional Golfers Association (PGA) tournament, is one of the premier golf courses in the world.

The Hebrew word for pebble or stone is *ehven*. *Ehven*, which is comprised of only three Hebrew letters, *aleph*, *vet* and *nun* (אבן), is itself a combination of two words: *av* (אב) and *ben* (בן). *Av* means "father" and *ben* means "son." The PGA openly promotes the father-son relationship by holding an annual tournament in which partnerships of fathers-professional golfers and their amateur golfer sons compete against one other.

Raising a Tiger
What It Means to Be a Jewish Father

"Be strong as a tiger...to do the will of your Father in Heaven."
(*Ethics of Our Fathers* 5:23)

In September 1992, an experience, although not dramatic, changed the direction of my life. As my first child, Max, had been born three weeks before, it was actually a rather common experience for a "thirtysomething"-year-old American, college-educated father. Its impact, however, was no less profound.

One night I returned home from my synagogue study around midnight. Normally my late night returns home are not the source of comment, since my wife, Marilyn, is nearly always asleep by that time. However, this was not the case on that evening. Not only was Marilyn awake, but so was "Little Max."

Upset with me, Marilyn voiced her displeasure. Little Max sided with his mother. "Why are you so upset?" I asked my spouse. "After all, I was **only working** late."

My wife responded, "I love you and am supportive of what you do, although I wouldn't mind seeing you more often myself. However, I will **not** tolerate our dear, precious son to grow up without a father present!"

Exhausted, and knowing that I would awake early the next morning, I went straight to bed. However, Marilyn's remarks really made their mark. I could not fall asleep until after 2 a.m.

When Marilyn Quayle's husband — our former Vice President — spoke about the importance of a child growing up with a father around, I was among those like Murphy Brown and the United States' population who laughed at what he said. When Marilyn Gordon — the Rabbi's wife — spoke about similar "family values," I cried.

While I lay awake in bed, many thoughts passed through my mind. Interspersed with my thoughts were the lyrics of one of my favorite songs, *Cat's in the Cradle*, co-written by the late Harry Chapin.

Cat's in the Cradle traces the relationship between a father and the son who emulates him. Unfortunately, despite the father's great love for his son, he never seems to have enough time to spend with his growing boy. As the lyrics continue, we learn that the admiring son indeed does become just like his father — although not in a desirable fashion. When the father finally has the time to spend with his son, his now adult son is simply too busy. After the son rejects the father's offer to spend time with him, the song ends with the father's lament.

> And as I hung up the phone, it occurred to me,
> He'd grown up just like me.
> My boy was just like me.[1]

As I lay awake that fall night, I began to realize that in my three short weeks as a father, I was mirroring the mistakes of the father in the song. I was always too busy with other important matters, always promising to spend time with my son, but rarely delivering on my promises. This late night experience inspired me that *Rosh Hashanah* to resolve that I would spend more time with my family.

Not only is caring for and spending time with our children important in American culture, but it is endorsed in Jewish tradition as well.

In the *Book of Numbers*, Moses instructs the Tribes of Reuben and Gad to participate with the rest of their brothers in conquering the Land of Israel. They would be granted permission to settle on the Transjordan only once they ensured the well being of their families.

In the *Torah*, the first commandment specifically given to men is known as *p'riya u-r'viya* (procreation), to *"Be fruitful and multiply and fill up the land"* (*Genesis* 1:28).

Jewish tradition not only directs men to give life to children, but to spend plenty of time with their children. In addition to quantity, this time should be of high quality, or what I refer to as **Jewish Quality Time**.

The parent-child relationship is very special in Jewish tradition and is based upon the *mitzvah* of *Talmud Torah* (Jewish education) which falls ultimately upon the parents. This is a most important *mitzvah* since all parents, Rabbis and other teachers of *Torah* are viewed as agents of God in transmitting the teachings of Judaism to children, and must be treated with the utmost honor and respect.

The *mitzvah* of honoring one's parents (*kibbud av v'em*) extends to the time when the children are adults, and applies even after a person's parents have passed away. For example, a son is obligated to recite *Kaddish* for his parents after their deaths. Children especially honor the memory of parents on their *yahrtzeits* and at all *Yizkor* (memorial) services, as well as by giving *tzedaka*.

Just as children have obligations towards their parents, Jewish law is clear that, in addition to serving as positive role models parents are obligated to perform certain duties towards their children. One of these is spending Jewish Quality Time. Providing a traditional Jewish education to one's children is a parent's primary duty. In this regard, the *Talmud* states:

> Regarding his son, a father is obligated to circumcise him, redeem him, teach him *Torah*, find him a suitable wife, and teach him a craft; and according to some authorities, also to teach him how to swim.
>
> (*Kiddushin* 29a)

Each obligation deserves a closer examination:

1. *"Circumcise...him."* Circumcision (*brit milah/bris*; literally, "covenant") is the formal introduction of a Jewish male child into the Jewish community. The *mitzvah* is the obligation of the father, which he can, and should, delegate to a qualified *mohel*. Abraham, the first Hebrew father, circumcised his own son Isaac.

2. *"Redeem...him."* Based upon *Exodus* 13:13 and *Numbers* 18:16, in most instances, on the 31st day after birth, the father is obligated to redeem his firstborn son. This *mitzvah* is known as *pidyon ha-ben* and is performed

since originally, prior to the sin of the Golden Calf, the firstborn Israelite sons belonged to the service of God. This is another religious activity through which the father helps ensure full acceptance in the Jewish community for his son.

3. *"Teach him Torah."* The best way to ensure that our children continue our traditions is by teaching them *Torah*. Although a father is allowed to delegate the responsibility of Jewish education to teachers and schools, the lessons taught by our Jewish schools are best learned when reinforced at home. One of the most beautiful and worthwhile activities a father and his children can participate in is studying *Torah* at the children's level.

4. *"Find him a suitable wife."* It is important that we marry not only for love but also in order to perpetuate Judaism. It is crucial that a parent instill in his children the need to marry someone who will serve as a partner in promoting the values of the *Torah* and ensuring the survival of the Jewish people.

5. *"Teach him a craft."* *Parnasah,* the ability to earn a livelihood, is critical in Jewish tradition. We must help guide each of our children to a fulfilling career that will enable them to raise a family as well as to contribute to the Jewish community.

6. *"Teach him how to swim."* Water covers a large portion of the world. Teaching our children how to survive both physically and emotionally is a critical life lesson.

In the name of *Rabbi Yehuda ben Tema,* the *Talmud* teaches:

> Be strong as a tiger, light as an eagle, swift as a gazelle, and mighty as a lion to do the will of your Father in Heaven.
>
> (*Ethics of Our Fathers* 5:23)

This statement, along with many others from *Ethics of Our Fathers,* provides a guide as to how we should lead our lives in order to reach our ultimate goal as Jews — to carry out the will of God. Similarly, this statement provides us with a road map as to how parents should encourage their children to behave.

"Strong as a tiger." According to the great Sage the *Bartenura*, this statement teaches that a student should never be ashamed of (repeatedly) asking his teacher about information he does not fully understand. The *Ba-al ha-Turim* explains that a Jew should be as "strong as a tiger" in that he should stand up to those who mock the *Torah*.

In the world of golf, the tiger has also become a most important symbol. The success of Eldrick "Tiger" Woods has helped reinforce such lessons as the importance of dedication and devotion in pursuing our dreams, and the importance of ascending above the color of one's skin. A lesson which has received much focus in the Tiger Woods story is the special value that a father can have influencing the life of his son.

The unique father-son relationship of Earl Woods and his mega superstar son has received a plethora of media attention. This special relationship is also the subject of a book co-authored by Earl Woods, entitled *Training a Tiger: A Father's Guide to Raising a Winner in Both Golf and Life*. Using golf as "his religion," Earl Woods shares with the reader his secrets on how he, along with his wife Kultida, raised a secure, bright, thoughtful son, who has also turned out to be a golfing legend.

"I was using golf to teach him about life," said Earl Woods in a 1997 issue of *People Weekly*, "About how to handle responsibility and pressure."[2]

Like Harry Chapin, Earl Woods also strongly promotes the importance of quality time spent with children. In the elder Woods' own words as he shares in his book:

> A parent should make time to spend with the child. It is not always easy in this age of two-job households, but I believe time is a product of one's desires and priorities. If your priority is your child, you will find time. And it will be quality time because the child knows the difference between thoughtful answers and offhanded remarks. You must always be aware that you are conveying to your child that you care. Offer direction and guidance, too, in small doses initially and always fairly and compassionately.[3]

The special attention given to him by his father has not only helped Tiger become a great success in golf, but a great success in life as well. As a result of their strong relationship, there exists a special bond between Tiger and his devoted, loving father.

Love and respect between father and son are not just found in the world of golf. On New Year's day in 1998, quarterback Brian Griese led the Michigan Wolverines to a 21-16 Rose Bowl victory over Washington State. One of the Rose Bowl television broadcasters was Brian's father, Hall of Fame quarterback, Bob Griese. On national television, in front of millions of viewers worldwide, both Brian and Bob expressed their great, mutual love and respect. Bob lost his wife to cancer when Brian was 12, and he raised Brian and his brothers as a single parent.

Just like Earl Woods, Bob Griese, and Harry Chapin, Jewish tradition also strongly encourages parent-child bonding. It is imperative that we spend as much Jewish Quality Time as possible with our children. We must engage with them in such activities as:

- helping with their homework (both Jewish and secular studies);
- attending synagogue programs;
- playing sports;
- sharing a *Shabbat* dinner together as a family; and
- ...if our children are young, teaching them as the Chapin song says — about "Little boy blue and the man in the moon."!

We must spend as much Jewish Quality Time with our children as possible. Peter Lynch, the former manager of the Fidelity Magellan Fund, said: "Nobody on his deathbed ever said, 'I wish I'd spent more time at the office.'"[4]

Since I resolved to spend more time with my family, my wife and I have been blessed with two more children. Life has become busier both at home and outside our home.

Have I accomplished my goal? Yes and no. I have, but not to a degree with which I am completely satisfied.

My own daily schedule, typical of many, is an overwhelming one. There are simply not enough hours in the day to accomplish everything on time, according to my own standards. Therefore, slowly, I have learned how to prioritize. Spending Jewish Quality Time with my family ranks as a top priority. In addition to participating in such important activities like playing catch with my children, reviewing their studies (both Jewish and secular) with them, and attending important school events, I have made a decision that certain times each day are "family times." These are times which will be disrupted only by **real** emergencies. These "family times" rank as the most important parts of my day.

There is a powerful concept in Judaism known as *teshuva* (repentance). *Teshuva* connotes growth and improvement. It directs every Jew to strive daily to become a better person, a better son or daughter, a better mother or father.

A father fulfilling the *mitzvah* of *p'riya u-r'viya* is a personal matter, but one which is ultimately controlled by God. However, spending time with our children and whether this time constitutes Jewish Quality Time is an issue which ultimately is within our own control.

Each of us must do all we can to prevent ourselves from becoming like the father in *Cat's in the Cradle* — always too busy to spend time with his child. We must strive to become a positive role model like Earl Woods is to Tiger and Bob Griese is to Brian.

The Prophet *Malakhi* (3:24) stated: "And He [God] shall turn the heart of the fathers towards their sons and the heart of the sons towards their fathers." By making this prophecy a reality, Jewish men will truly fulfill the lesson of What It Means to Be a Jewish Father.

CHAPTER 6

SPORTS AGENCY
A Season for Silence and Speaking

"…a season to be silent and a season to speak."
(*Ecclesiastes* 3:7)

When I was a child, most professional athletes spoke directly to team management in negotiating the terms of their own contracts. Few, if any, players and coaches today fail to engage an agent to represent them in contract negotiations. The sports agent, in effect, advises the sports figure-client when it is appropriate to be silent and when to speak. Along with the expansion of free agency and other recent "pro-player" legal achievements, the use of agents has caused player salaries to rise tremendously and vastly improve player benefits. For such "indiscretions," sports agents have received a "bad rap" by many fans.

Absolutely Yes!
I Am My Brother's Keeper!

After Cain murdered his brother Abel, God inquired of Cain, "Where is Abel, your brother?"

The rather arrogant but guilty Cain responded, "I do not know; am I my brother's keeper?" (*Genesis* 4:9)

Although God chose not to respond directly to Cain's remark, had He done so, His response would most likely have been something to the effect of, "Absolutely yes! You are your brother's keeper!"

Not only is causing harm to your brother against Jewish tradition, but to the contrary, our tradition commands us to be proactive in helping others in all ways.

Jewish tradition serves as the model for all cultures and societies in reaching out and caring for others. Monetary acts of caring are known as *tzedaka*. Non-monetary acts of caring are known as *gemilut ḥasadim*. *Gemilut ḥasadim* (acts of loving kindness) are a special category of God's commandments (*mitzvot*). They include the *mitzvot* of visiting the sick (*bikkur ḥolim*) and comforting the bereaved (*niḥum avel*). These acts of kindness are reminders of the importance of the role of individuals as well as of a community in helping others in times of need.

Assisting those in financial need is so important that it is not simply enough to give charity when one is moved to do so, rather *tzedaka* (literally, "justice") is a mandated activity. It is a *mitzvah*, a commandment.

The leading authority on *tzedaka* is Maimonides (*Rambam*) (1135-1204 C.E.). In his dual roles as Rabbi and physician, Maimonides strongly promoted the importance of helping others. In his code of Jewish law — the *Mishneh Torah*, the *Rambam* devotes an entire section to *tzedaka* and other forms of helping those in need. Maimonides teaches that the main objectives of *tzedaka* include not only ensuring the financial well-being of the person who is in need, but also doing so in the most sensitive, *menschlikhkite* manner. Using these objectives as his guide, Maimonides ranks the highest level of *tzedaka* as not necessarily an outright gift, but rather a way to help ensure that the person in need is made self-sufficient.

In the words of Maimonides:

> There are eight levels of charity, each one higher than the other. The highest level, for which there is none greater, is when one strengthens the hand of a poor Jew and gives him a gift or [an] [interest-free] loan or forms a partnership with him or finds work for him in order to strengthen him so that he no longer needs to ask from other people...
> (Maimonides, *Mishneh Torah*, *Hilkhot Matanot la-Evyonim* 10:7)

Not only has our Jewish tradition historically served as a role model to other societies for the proper legislation and theoretical education of charity, but it has served and continues to serve as a model for its practical application of *tzedaka* as well.

During the days of the *Talmud*, under the supervision of trusted community leaders (*gabbaim*) various funds were established and administered to ensure that those in need received proper care. Such funds included a general fund (*kupah*), a clothing fund, a food pantry (*tamhui*), and a fund for interest-free loans (*gemilut hasadim* society). In contemporary North American communities, various not-for-profit Jewish organizations serve in a similar capacity.

An integral component of the Jewish school curriculum is to teach students of all ages the importance of *tzedaka*. Along those lines, I am reminded of the time I was leaving rather hurriedly our local *kosher* bakery accompanied by my daughter Rita, then four years old. Many Jewish establishments promote *tzedaka* by leaving *tzedaka* containers (*pushkehs*) on their counters. That day after paying for my bakery order, the attendant handed me my change. In my haste, I placed the change in my pocket. When Rita saw what I did with the change, she said in a soft, kind voice, "Daddy, I have to tell you something."

Rushed, I responded, "Not now Ritie, I'm in a hurry."

Rita wouldn't let me leave the bakery until she spoke her mind! She repeated, "Daddy, I have to tell you something."

I bent over to hear Rita very respectfully whisper into my ear, "Daddy, you forgot to give *tzedaka.*"

Now no matter how much of in a hurry I may be, I never leave a store with *pushkehs* without first giving *tzedaka.*

The proper response to Cain's retort is a resounding, "Yes! We are our brother's keeper!" This response is further reinforced by the *Talmudic* statement, "...all Jews must serve as guarantors for each other" (*"Kol Yisrael areivim zeh ba-zeh"*) (*Shevuot* 39a).

Serving as "our brother's keeper" has a universal message and one which transcends the Jewish community. All societies and cultures must designate as a top priority caring for the less fortunate and those in need.

Throughout the years, countless athletes have been actively involved in reaching out and helping those in need. Here are a few examples:

- A journeyman baseball player in the 1960s and '70s, Hank Allen was able to qualify for Major League Baseball's pension plan, in part, because of the kindness of his superstar brother, Dick "Richie" Allen. As a member of the White Sox, Dick Allen successfully lobbied the Sox management to allow Hank to be a member of the team's official roster in order to officially qualify him for the pension.[1] In spite of his controversial reputation, Dick Allen fulfilled the sports version of serving as his "brother's keeper." He also exemplified a universal manifestation of Maimonides' highest level of *tzedaka* by ensuring Hank's livelihood. In recent years, brother Hank has helped return the favor by providing Dick the opportunity to train thoroughbred horses at the stable belonging to him and his other brother, Ron.[2]

- Headed by announcer and former Major League catcher, Joe Garagiola, the Baseball Assistance Team ("BAT") is dedicated to assisting former ballplayers who have encountered hard times. BAT has assisted those who suffer from problems such as drug and alcohol abuse. It has also helped pay funeral and medical expenses for the downtrodden members of the baseball community.

- Many professional athletes have used their wealth to establish foundations to assist the less fortunate. When the Bears cut defensive tackle Chris Zorich in October, 1997, there was great dismay among the fans, not only because of Zorich's value to the team as a player, but also for his heartfelt dedication to the Chicago community. As a native Chicagoan, Zorich wanted to show his appreciation to the community by establishing the Christopher Zorich Foundation. This foundation is dedicated to helping those in need and since its inception in 1993, the Christopher Zorich Foundation has assisted over 40,000 needy families. "The image of Zorich...as he personally makes holiday food-drive deliveries is likely to outlast his image in a football helmet," wrote *Chicago Tribune* columnist, Eric Zorn commenting on Zorich's community outreach.[3]

- Leigh Steinberg, a highly respected sports agent and well-known philanthropist in California, was the model and inspiration for the movie *Jerry Maguire*. In addition to looking out for the financial and overall well-being of his clients, Steinberg insists that his clients establish foundations and other programs that will benefit society. Steinberg's childhood was spent being raised in a household which stressed the importance of helping others:

> ..."To this day..." says Leigh, "...if I walked home and told my dad I'd negotiated a $10 million contract he'd just say, 'Gee that's great.' But if I told him I had set up a community program that helped kids, he'd throw his arms around me and really get excited. Because of that, I had to make a difference somehow..."[4]

These are just a few of many lesser-known stories of how sports figures have reached out to help others in need. Other players have participated in worthy causes like establishing safe after-school programs for children, visiting the sick, establishing college scholarships, and sending a medical mission to Kenya.

Being our "brother's keeper" reminds us that we must always be ready and willing to assist anyone who is in need. Whether it is performing the great *mitzvah* of visiting the sick, comforting a person after the death of a loved one, or by giving *tzedaka* monies, we always must be acutely aware of the plight of others.

When it comes to being our "brother's keeper," we must learn not to be like Cain. When it comes to *tzedaka* and *gemilut hasadim*, Judaism's formulas for being our "brother's keeper," we must learn from the benevolent acts and teachings of Maimonides and emulate the acts of such leading sports figures as Joe Garagiola, Dick Allen, Chris Zorich and Leigh Steinberg.

"Am I my brother's keeper?" "Absolutely, yes! I am my brother's keeper!"

Jerry Maguire and the Rabbis

"Show me the money!" shouts Tom Cruise as sports agent Jerry Maguire in the 1997 movie, *Jerry Maguire*. In trying to retain the services of his NFL receiver-client Rod Tidwell, Maguire epitomizes the greed of the sports agency world by promoting money over well-being.

While visiting another client, a severely injured hockey player in the hospital, the player's son lashes out at Maguire, accusing him of only seeming to care about money. The agent's sole concern is for his client to be well enough, quick enough, to resume his lucrative career as a professional hockey player.

The young boy, however, is only concerned about his father's health and recovery.

This event in the hospital serves as a catalyst for Maguire to re-evaluate his role as a sports agent, and he decides to promote the idea that the agent must serve as a sincerely caring friend, as well as one who looks out for both the financial and spiritual well-being of the athlete-client and his family.

Instead of embracing Maguire and his new found beliefs, Maguire's agency fires him. The unemployed Maguire leaves his former employer with only one client — Rod Tidwell.

It is the movie's irony that Jerry Maguire was only able to retain Tidwell as his sole client after first repeatedly shouting "Show me the money!" Although the outwardly flashy aging receiver for the Arizona Cardinals pressures Maguire to repeatedly chant this phrase, it is he who ultimately teaches Maguire the "real" value of money. Maguire, in turn, teaches Tidwell the "real" value of an agent. In addition to serving as negotiator and financial manager, Maguire learns to serve as a friend, advisor and caregiver to his clients. Tidwell teaches Maguire that the main purpose of "the money" is to take care of one's family and to ensure their financial security and well-being.

Jerry Maguire, who is modeled after real-life sports agent Leigh Steinberg, serves as a model for all sports agents. Instead of simply serving the needs of one's client primarily for personal financial gains, the agent must best serve the needs of the client and his family, regardless of the magnitude of the agent's own monetary benefits.

Many sports agents are trained attorneys and the stereotypical behavior of the "non-Maguire like" sports agents further promote the negative stereotype of attorneys. A congregant once asked me, "How many lawyer jokes are there in the world?" He responded, "There are really only three; the rest are all true stories!"[5]

Attorneys, unfortunately, have been the target of many jokes. On the contrary, through their public service through the years, attorneys have made major contributions to our society. In many democratic countries it has been the attorneys who have led, organized, motivated, rallied, sacrificed and promoted justice, morality and order. David T. Link, Dean Emeritus of the University of Notre Dame Law School, writes that throughout history political leaders who wanted to subordinate the rule of law in a given society, first sought to subordinate the influence of the lawyers.[6]

The practice of law is ultimately a service-oriented profession. The role of the attorney is to zealously represent his client and to, ultimately, take care of the client's needs.

"Show me the money!"

According to Jewish tradition, if used properly money can be most spiritual. In addition to giving *tzedaka* (charity) monies to help those in need, and using them to build and maintain institutions vital to the Jewish community, the ability to earn money as a means of livelihood (*parnasah*) is critical.

The *Talmud* (*Beitza* 32b) teaches, "Anyone who depends on the table of others (for financial support), the world appears dark for him." Along similar lines, the *Talmud* (*Ethics of Our Fathers* 3:21) states, "*Im ein kemah ein Torah,*" or "If there is no sustenance, there is no *Torah*."

In addition to physicians and other professional providers of care, the spiritual caregivers are Rabbis, who provide care through teaching, religious counsel and serving the pastoral needs of the congregants.

In order for a Rabbi to adequately care for the needs of his constituents, it is critical that the Rabbi be able to first provide for the financial well-being and security of his family. At the same time, he must not compromise his position as a caregiver for his congregants.

How can this best be achieved? A well-drafted contract which provides for the financial and spiritual well-being of the Rabbi is one essential device to help achieve these objectives. Rabbis and other Jewish community professionals should be represented during their contract negotiations by high caliber attorneys, who are sensitive to the needs of the Jewish community and to its leaders. This can best be achieved by bringing in the "Jerry Maguires" of the legal/Rabbinic world!

It is both impractical and unfeasible for a Rabbi to represent himself in contract negotiations, either in drafting or in other matters related to the Rabbinic contract. In contractual matters, the Rabbi is usually outmatched both in terms of the numbers and skills of the negotiators. Even if the Rabbi is highly sophisticated in contract negotiations and in other pertinent financial matters, an individual representing himself often times is too emotionally involved which can jeopardize the success of the negotiations.

There is a familiar old adage proclaiming that, "A man who is his own lawyer has a fool as a client." This applies to members of the clergy as well. Furthermore, if a Rabbi "out negotiates" the synagogue's negotiations team, it could lead to great resentment from his congregants. Since the Rabbi has a very sacred relationship with the congregation, his role as spiritual leader, educator and religious counselor could be compromised. In this case, the dignity of the office of the Rabbi could be impaired.

Traditionally, Rabbis usually approach their employment contract negotiations in four ways:

1. By themselves, without any input or involvement from any legal counsel;

2. By themselves, but with input from an attorney who has no direct contact with the synagogue negotiators;

3. "Representation" by an attorney who is a congregant sympathetic to the needs of the Rabbi; and

4. Representation by a skilled independent attorney who is not a member of the Rabbi's congregation, but is retained by the Rabbi.

From both a theoretical and practical standpoint, representation by a non-congregant attorney achieves the best financial and professional benefits for the Rabbi and his family.

Many Rabbis do in fact involve attorneys, but they are usually behind the scenes and not visibly, actively involved in the negotiations. Their main role has been to review a contract and to prevent any major damage from occurring. In essence, it appears — in many cases — the attorney is doing the Rabbi a favor. This creates the misperception among the lay leadership of the synagogue that most Rabbis do not even want attorney representation!

The best way to remove the focus from Rabbis, who retain an attorney for contract negotiations and other contractual matters, is to mainstream and popularize this concept.

With these thoughts in mind, in November, 1994, The Decalogue Society of Lawyers, a Chicago-based Jewish bar association, established a committee known as The Decalogue Project for Jewish Community Professionals and Institutions. One goal of The Decalogue Project is to create a more harmonious relationship between the community, its lay leaders and Jewish community professionals to enable the community to reach its potential more readily. One way to help achieve this objective is by actively caring for our caregivers, the Rabbis and other Jewish community professionals. In this spirit, The Decalogue Project created a Lawyer Referral Service to provide attorneys, who are sensitive to the needs of the Jewish community and its leaders, to represent Rabbis and others in contract negotiations and in other contractual matters. The Decalogue Project strives to recruit and train the "Jerry Maguires" of the American Jewish legal community.[7]

Like Jerry Maguire and other altruistic sports agents, the role of the contract representative for Rabbis and other Jewish community professionals is to help ensure the financial and professional well-being of his client.

In the words of our Sage Hillel:

> If I am not for myself, who is for me?
> When I am for myself only, what am I?
> And if not now, when?

(*Ethics of Our Fathers* 1:14)

CHAPTER 7

THE OLYMPICS
A Season for Peace

"...a season for peace."
(*Ecclesiastes* 3:8)

For about four weeks every four years, nations come together peacefully to compete in sports. The Olympics give us the opportunity to view a manifestation similar to how the world will be after the arrival of the *Mashiaḥ* (Messiah). As the prophet Micah points out "...nation will not lift up sword against nation and they will not learn war anymore" (*Micah* 4:3). The prophet Isaiah adds, during Messianic times, "...a wolf will dwell with a lamb..." (*Isaiah* 11:6).

Rabbi Zusya Strikes Out
Take Me Out of the Ball Game

In February, 1994, United States Olympic figure skater Nancy Kerrigan returned home from the Olympic games in Lilliehammer with a silver medal. Because of her accomplishments on the ice, the American public bestowed her with tremendous adulation and great financial rewards. She received endorsement offers, opportunities to appear on major television shows, and even a trip to Disneyworld!

On the other hand, her teammate and arch rival, Tonya Harding, returned home to a hostile American public and to threats of imminent disciplinary hearings and legal proceedings for her alleged role in the physical assault of Kerrigan.[1]

Why was the American public so absorbed with the clubbing of Nancy Kerrigan and her rivalry with Ms. Harding? One reason may be that competition is so much a part of American life that each of us can relate to this story in some way.

Competition is a major factor in all aspects of our lives. We face competition in the professional world, in sports, in social settings and in academics. The Kerrigan-Harding relationship, however, epitomizes the ultimate dark side of competition.

My experience with sports, both as a fan and as a participant, have influenced my life in a positive way. As a fan, I find relaxation in viewing sporting events or news accounts of sporting events, and it also allows me to participate more effectively in social conversation. As a participant, sports have helped reinforce such important Jewish real life lessons as sportsmanship, physical fitness and teamwork. However, as a participant and as an observer, I have also seen how sports can teach real life negative lessons or how *not* to be.

Recently I received a copy of a letter written by the disciplinary committee of a local youth baseball league and sent to all area baseball managers. This letter, in part, reads:

> Dear Managers,
>
> Regrettably, a situation has recently taken place in the league, whereby two boys began fighting while they were going through the congratulatory line. One boy was suspended for two weeks and the other was suspended for one game.
>
> The real tragedy is that these boys are only eight years old. They are reflecting a lot of the actions demonstrated by our older players.

I agree with the contents of this letter and would propose only one change. I would change the sentence which reads "they are reflecting a lot of the actions demonstrated by our older players" to read instead, "they are reflecting a lot of the actions demonstrated by our older players and encouraged by far too many parents in our community."

Accompanying this letter was an article entitled *Give Young Athletes a Fair Shake*, published in *Sports Illustrated*. In this article, the writer places the blame on the adults involved. To emphasize this point, Dennis Sullivan, Director of Communications for Little League Baseball stated, "Sportsmanship is not a difficult lesson for a child to learn. But sometimes it's a difficult lesson for an adult to teach."[2]

On a recent television program, a prominent psychology professor suggested that the way to help correct the problem of unsportsmanlike behavior in organized school and youth sports leagues is to require the adult coaches to go through a course on how to coach youth more effectively.

This television segment pointed out that 50 percent of American youth who are enrolled in organized sports leagues drop out by age 12. Instead of saying, "take me out *to* the ball game," more and more of our children are saying, "take me out *of* the ball game."

What does our Jewish tradition teach about competition? One of my favorite stories is one which involves the highly acclaimed and revered Rabbi *Meshulam Zusya* of Hanipoli, a *Ḥasidic* Rabbi who lived in the 1700s.

When he was late in his years, Rabbi Zusya became very introspective about his imminent death. One day, noticing that he was unusually despondent, his students tried reassuring their beloved *Rebbe* that he had a secure place in the "world to come" (*olam ha-bah*).

"*Rebbe*, you shouldn't worry," his students told him. "After all, you have the patience of Rabbi Hillel, the wisdom of King Solomon, the humility of Moses and the kindness of Abraham."

Rabbi *Zusya* replied, "I am not worried about how I will respond when confronted by God's angels and asked, 'Why weren't you like Rabbi Hillel? Why weren't you like King Solomon? Why weren't you like Moses? Why weren't you like Abraham?' But, I am concerned as to how I will respond when asked, 'Why weren't you like *Zusya*?'"

According to the flavor of Jewish tradition, the appropriate questions we must ask regarding competition are not:

- "Why am I *not* as good a skater as Nancy Kerrigan?"
- "Why isn't my child as good a baseball player as is my next door neighbor's child?"
- "Why aren't I as wealthy as is my best friend from high school?"

According to Jewish tradition, the appropriate questions we need to ask are:

- "Why haven't I tried my hardest?"
- "Why haven't I strived to achieve my potential?"
- "Why weren't you like *Zusya*?"

Trying our best and striving to reach our potential is not only the "Rabbi *Zusya* Principle," but it is also what *teshuva* (repentance) is all about. *Teshuva*, repentance or return, is an activity that we are supposed to practice daily throughout our lives and with greater concentration during the High Holy Day season.

According to the great *Sephardic* physician and Rabbi, Maimonides (*Rambam*), proper *teshuva* includes the following steps performed by the person who has sinned:

1) recognizing that what he did was wrong (*hakarat ha-ḥet*);

2) confession (*vidui*); and

3) not committing the same sin again (*kabala l'ha-ba*).

In order for Maimonides' formula for *teshuva* to be successful, Rabbi Zusya's Principle must be applied in full; a truly penitent person is one who tries his best.

Jewish tradition urges us to try our hardest to reach our potential as Jews by returning to the ways of God, the ways of the *Torah*. The Rabbis teach us that a person should even perform *teshuva* on the day he dies. Of course, since we do not know the exact day we die, everyday is the best time for *teshuva*.

One of the best illustrations of *teshuva* and the Rabbi Zusya Principle can be found in the fictional character from the movie *Forrest Gump*. Forrest Gump, a man with a lower than average I.Q., shows in Hollywood fairy tale fashion that with the proper support from loved ones, an individual *can* achieve greatness — provided that he tries his hardest to reach his potential. Forrest Gump succeeds in life because he follows the advice of his loving mother — *not* to compete against others, but to compete only with his own potential.

In the world of sports, one of the best illustrations of the Rabbi Zusya Principle is the competition between Mark McGwire and Sammy Sosa in 1998. That year, McGwire and Sosa each broke the single season record for home runs set by Yankee great Roger Maris in 1961.

Sammy Peralta Sosa comes from San Pedro de Macoris. This Dominican Republic town has produced numerous Major League Baseball players. Sosa grew up very poor, shining shoes and washing cars to help support his family. Mark David McGwire comes from a more privileged background, growing up in California and attending the University of Southern California. McGwire participated in the Olympic games in 1984 as a member of the United States baseball team.

In spite of their diverse backgrounds, they shared a desire to break Maris' coveted record and both were model competitors. Instead of jeering each other, they engaged in cheering for one another. The "friendly competition" helped each player in his successful pursuit of the magical number 61.

Both Sammy Sosa and Mark McGwire incorporated the Rabbi Zusya Principle of competition; instead of competing against each other, these two great sluggers ultimately competed against their own potential. At the end of the 1998 baseball season, both stars shattered Roger Maris' mark of 61 as McGwire hit 70 and Sosa 66 home runs![3]

In the academic forum, the Rabbi Zusya Principle and *teshuva* teach us to encourage our children to study their hardest and then to accept their grades. In the world of sports, it teaches us to encourage our children to play their best, to be happy and to always exemplify sportsmanlike conduct. It teaches us to skate against our best rather than compete against the "Kerrigans" and "Hardings." It teaches us to compete with our own potential. It teaches us to compete in a positive, sportsmanlike, *menschlikhkite* fashion like Mark McGwire and Sammy Sosa.

As Jews, *teshuva* and the Rabbi Zusya Principle teach us that we should always try to improve the level of our interactions with our fellow human beings and with God. It teaches us that we should always be open to learn more about our tradition, in order to help us and our children become even better Jews. It teaches us that it is critical that we do all that we can to encourage our children to participate in such activities as Jewish day school and youth programs. The Rabbi Zusya Principle and *teshuva* teach us that we should do all that we can to increase our level of the performance of the *mitzvot* (God's commandments). It teaches us to get more involved in synagogue and Jewish life.

We must work our hardest so that we may reach our potential as Jews, thus ensuring that Rabbi Zusya hits a "home run" and does not "strike out."

CHAPTER 8

LEADERS AND HEROES
A Season for Loving and Hating

"A season to love and a season to hate…"
(*Ecclesiastes* 3:8)

Rabbis and leaders of the sports community share many of the qualities necessary for effective leadership. It is these Jewish leaders that we should look to emulate and serve as role models. We must look for heroes within the confines of the Jewish community: in our homes, among our Rabbis, and among other contemporary leaders and great Jewish leaders of history.

Follow the Leaders
Rabbis, Coaches and Commissioners

"*Ben Zoma* says: Who is wise?
One who learns from all people..."

(Ethics of Our Fathers 4:1)

"Keep an open mind" is sound advice. One must listen to what others say, think about their advice and, if it makes sense, follow it. This is what helps make us better parents, better spouses, better friends and better professionals.

When we seek advice about how to better ourselves in our various professional fields, the best resources are our colleagues, particularly those senior to us in knowledge and experience. We can also learn from the successes and failures of professionals in other fields.

The role of a pulpit Rabbi is multi-faceted. Rabbis are teachers, scholars, deciders of law, writers, officiants at services, administrators, comforters and champions of the downtrodden, and advisors to the young and the old. **Rabbis are leaders**.

The best role models and teachers for Rabbis are other Rabbis. Each Rabbi can tell you which Rabbi inspired him to pursue the calling of the Rabbinate, who serves as his Rabbinic role model and which Rabbi is his mentor. Rabbis can also gain important insights from well-intentioned, respectful and supportive congregants. Rabbis can be enlightened by the successes and experiences of leaders in other professions such as political and civil rights leaders, and leaders of other religious communities.

A category to add to this list is — "leaders of the sports community." Rabbis, indeed, can learn from the successes of coaches, managers, general managers, owners and commissioners.

In many ways, the roles and duties of the American synagogue Rabbi incorporates the duties and roles of sports leaders. Like a successful coach, a Rabbi must be an effective teacher, listener, disciplinarian and motivator. He must be able to communicate effectively with management as well as with the community-at-large. Like a commissioner, he must be able to make all decisions only in the "best-interests of the game." For a Rabbi that "game" is Judaism. Like a coach, a Rabbi must be able to instill the value of team play, drive, and success in his constituents. He must be able to balance diverse personalities and resolve conflict. A Rabbi, like a coach, must be a strong leader. Only from a strong, unwavering leadership will he gain respect and become a role model to others.

One advantage of collegiate competition over professional sports is that the college coach has a greater likelihood of being an effective teacher and role model to his players. For many college athletes, the school is their first experience living away from their families. Many of these athletes miss their parents and have a great need for guidance. In many cases, a "father and son" type of relationship may develop between a coach and his players.

Some of the more notable coaches in college history have included Knute Rockne, the Chicago native who shaped a small Catholic university into a perennial national football power. Rockne is best remembered not just for his coaching innovations on the field, but also for his inspiring pep talks. Former President Ronald Reagan, who played the movie character George Gipper in *Knute Rockne: All American,* helped highlight Rockne's inspirational/ motivational skills when his character was the subject of Rockne's "Win one for the Gipper" locker room pep talk.

Along with guiding his congregants through the daily rituals of Jewish life, the Rabbi also must constantly supplement this role with "pep talks." These words of inspiration come in the form of formal sermons, remarks made while teaching classes, and impromptu insights offered in private meetings. Inspiring words, along with proper follow-up and support, can motivate a person to raise his level of observance and spirituality.

One of the most successful coaches in college history remains the legendary John Wooden. During a 12 year span at UCLA, Wooden, also known as "the Wizard of Westwood," led his basketball Bruins to an unprecedented 10 NCAA National Championships. Particularly impressive was that the highly disciplined Wooden was able to win most of these championships during a time of great political unrest in America. In a time when American youth mistrusted their leadership, Wooden was able to discipline his players and teach them that the path to victory was best achieved by focusing on playing the fundamentals of the game. Many of Wooden's players matriculated to not only successful NBA careers, but to careers as leaders who advocated strong "off-the-court" ideals.

The successful Rabbi must act like Coach John Wooden and teach his congregants the fundamentals of the synagogue, community and Jewish tradition. The Rabbi must assist his congregants in meeting their problems directly and addressing them in the proper fashion.

The Hebrew word for "sons" is *banim*. *Banim* is also used when referring to students. In Jewish tradition, the respect a student owes his Rabbi and other teachers of *Torah* sometimes even exceeds the respect that a son owes his own father. After all, both fathers and Rabbis are responsible for the education of their "sons" and both are greatly influential in the spiritual development of their students.

One afternoon, while watching a Chicago Bulls basketball game on television with my son, Max — then four years old, I pointed to Phil Jackson indicating that he was the Bulls coach. I asked Max if he knew what a coach was. He responded, "A coach is a teacher."

Another one of the most successful college coaches of all times is Joe Paterno, the Penn State Nittany Lions coach for more than 30 years. There is a famous Hebrew phrase which teaches that a person is just like their name, *"Ki khi-sh'mo ken hu"* (*Samuel I* 25:25). In Latin a father is known as *"pater."* Coach Paterno is like his name in that he has been a father-figure to many of his players. As a teacher, he not only instills in his players the importance of winning on-the-field, but off-the-field as well. Paterno stresses the value of education. It is well known to Penn State recruits that a major expectation of Coach Joe Paterno's program is that when his players finish their football careers at Penn State, they must leave the campus with at least a Bachelor's degree. Joe Paterno is a role model for other coaches when it comes to encouraging college student-players to earn degrees which will help ensure their professional success whether or not they make it in professional sports.

Like college coaches and their players, Rabbis have a captive audience with synagogue youth. Like Coach Paterno who has only four years to influence his players, Rabbis must take advantage of their relatively brief window of time to inspire our youth to succeed as adult Jews. The key to achieving this success is Jewish education.

Coaches serve not only as mentors and teachers to players, but to other coaches as well.

After serving as head coach of the North Carolina Tarheels, college basketball's most winning coach, Dean Smith retired in 1997. Smith recommended that his assistant for 30 years, Bill Guthridge, serve as his successor. The Dean Smith-Bill Guthridge professional relationship was a very open one, a relationship highlighted by two bright men sharing ideas and skills with each other. Because of their great relationship and their willingness to suppress unnecessary ego needs, the Tarheel program flourished under this joint leadership.

"... you don't get that in sports very often," Tarheel assistant coach Dave Hanners said in *Sports Illustrated*, "... someone who stays that long with you and doesn't want your job. And someone you can delegate that much to without him thinking he's the boss. They had a perfect marriage."[1]

The Rabbi's involvement in the selection of all professional synagogue personnel is one of his most important duties. The Rabbi, as "Chief Religious Officer" must be comfortable working with the synagogue's assistant Rabbi, Cantor, educational director, youth director and other professionals. Because of his training and experience, a Rabbi has the requisite knowledge to determine which professionals are best-suited for synagogue professional positions.

In 1997 while addressing a group of Rabbis in Chicago, world-renowned *Talmudic* scholar Rabbi Adin Steinsaltz said that, like a coach, a *Talmud* teacher must first have a thorough knowledge of his subject matter. A key component for a successful Rabbi and coach is to have a deep understanding of their respective subjects.

In sports, one may think that former star players make the best coaches, because, after all, they must have the greatest knowledge of the game since they achieved stardom. It is true that some star athletes have graduated to become outstanding coaches. John Wooden, for example, is the only person inducted in the Basketball Hall of Fame twice for his accomplishments as both a coach and a player. However, this is more the exception than the rule. Many star athletes are often unable to deal as successfully with the frustrations normally experienced by coaches. This may be because naturally talented players are less likely to experience frustrations as players and may not be exposed to higher levels of fundamental play. The reverse may also hold true. Many of the struggling players are forced to thoroughly examine the fundamentals of the game, as well as to consistently learn how to deal with frustration.

Baseball managers Tony LaRussa, Tommy Lasorda, Sparky Anderson and Walter Alston all had brief, undistinguished Major League playing careers. Alston, for example, was known in the minor leagues as a slugging first baseman, but actually only had one Major League at-bat. Having struggled as a player provides a manager with a greater opportunity to be a better, more patient teacher, allowing not only the ability to sympathize with a player, but also to empathize with him.

An effective Rabbinic leader must also be a patient teacher. He must not only thoroughly know his material, but also must be prepared to address all questions and issues. Rabbi Hillel taught, "...the shy person cannot learn, the temperamental person cannot teach" (*Ethics of Our Fathers* 2:6).

The professional life of a Rabbi can be compared to a roller coaster. It is consistently filled with great highs and tremendous lows. In the very same day, a Rabbi can help celebrate a *bris* or another family *simḥa* and then officiate at a funeral. Many Rabbis also constantly face petty political challenges within the synagogue community. The successful Rabbi, like the successful sports leader, will use the experiences gained from his own struggles to benefit the members of his community.

A key role of the Rabbi is to serve as the sole arbiter of Jewish law (*Marah d'Atrah*) in his synagogue community. He must be given the requisite opportunity to examine the law, and interpret it carefully so that Jewish tradition is not compromised and his interpretation best addresses the needs of his community. Unfortunately, with each decision, there are always going to be unhappy congregants. At times, some dissatisfied congregants will manifest their disapproval by opposing the Rabbi, thereby threatening his ability, both present and future, to serve as their Rabbi. Although the Rabbi's mission is to serve in the best interests of his community by protecting Jewish law and tradition, his job security is most tenuous.

In this regard, the office of the Rabbi is most similar to the office of the commissioner of a major league sport. The Commissioner of Major League Baseball is hired and fired by the owners of the baseball clubs. He is mandated by his "employers" to "act in the best interests of baseball." However, when the Commissioner's interpretation of baseball's best interests do not coincide with the definition shared by the majority of the owners, the Commissioner's job is often jeopardized.

In 1920, the first lone Commissioner of Major League Baseball, Judge Kenesaw Mountain Landis made it very clear to his employers that in order to succeed, he needed complete control. Landis, a federal judge, was hired by the baseball team owners in the wake of the 1919 Black Sox scandal, and the fall of the National Commission. Because of the control the owners provided him, Judge Landis was able to take bold actions which helped restore the respectability of the game of baseball. Even though a criminal jury acquitted the eight "Black Sox" players, Landis permanently banished these players from Organized Baseball. When he suspected wrongdoing by certain Major League teams, Landis declared that 200 of their players become free agents. Judge Kenesaw Mountain Landis served for 24 years as Baseball's Commissioner.

For synagogues to reach *their* greatest potential, Rabbis must be given full, unobstructed religious authority and control. After all, the Rabbi who renders a religious decision is not acting in his own best interests, but rather in the best interests of Jewish law and the community.

Another important duty of a college coach is to recruit top prep athletes for his team. The coach, in effect, controls who will play on his team. The most coveted job among professional coaches is to also serve as general manager, and thereby control all personnel decisions. In recent years, Rick Pitino and Pat Reilly entered into such arrangements with their NBA teams. Too often when a coach does not also serve as the team general manager, conflict arises between coach and management as to the selection and retention of players.

Likewise, in his role as "CRO," the Chief Religious Officer of the synagogue, the Rabbi must be active in every phase of the hiring process and must retain a veto power regarding all personnel matters. This will help ensure the selection and retention of top quality Jewish community professionals and individuals with whom the Rabbi is comfortable and who will help the Rabbi lead the congregation to higher levels of spirituality.

Legendary football coach Vince Lombardi, who lived by the famous phrase — "Winning isn't everything, it's the only thing" — was known as a strict disciplinarian who was not always popular with his players. Ultimately, however, he earned his players respect. In his book *Instant Replay*, former player Jerry Kramer said, "Lombardi was a cruel, kind, tough, gentle, miserable, wonderful man whom I often hate and often love and always respect."[2]

Even if unpopular, it is critical that a Rabbi always be respected and accorded the proper respect (*derekh eretz*) and honor (*kavod*). After all, "proper respect takes precedence [even] over the study of *Torah*" ("*Derekh eretz kadma la-Torah*").

In order for the World Jewish Community to survive and prosper, we must have highly qualified Rabbis to lead us; we must provide for ourselves Rabbis. Rabbis can be inspired by all kinds of individuals. In addition to fellow Rabbis, Rabbis can also gain important leadership insights from other leaders. Among these leaders are coaches, managers and commissioners.

Once we know that we are being led by qualified leaders, it is then important to incorporate into our lives the philosophy to — *Follow the Leaders: Rabbis, Coaches and Commissioners*.

Honor Your Father, Mother and Coach!
Derekh Eretz Kadma La-Torah

In the history of organized sports, there have been numerous incidents illustrating a lack of respect. Examples include players brawling with each other, fans verbally abusing players, overzealous protests against referee judgement calls, and disrespectful player conduct towards coaches. Unfortunately, no sport is immune from such unacceptable behavior. One of the most egregious cases ever involved NBA All-Star player Latrell Sprewell.

On December 1, 1997, Latrell Sprewell, then a guard on the Golden State Warriors,[3] flew into a rage during a practice session and choked his coach P. J. Carlesimo. Sprewell also threatened Carlesimo's life and punched him.[4]

To the credit of the Golden State Warriors and the National Basketball Association, the proper authorities immediately and swiftly meted out severe punishment to Sprewell. NBA Commissioner David Stern suspended Sprewell from the league for one year, which meant forfeiting millions of dollars. The Golden State Warriors terminated Sprewell's contract.

Both the NBA and the Golden State Warriors made a loud and clear statement to Sprewell and to the world, that a prerequisite to playing NBA basketball is to exhibit sportsmanlike behavior at all times. In the language of Jewish tradition they, in effect, proclaimed, "Proper respect takes precedence over basketball."

These punishments were subsequently reduced by an arbitrator who ruled, in part, that the Warriors must reinstate Sprewell's contract. The punishment ultimately received by Latrell Sprewell for his unacceptable behavior remains the most severe punishment ever meted out to a player in the history of team sports for an act unrelated to drugs or gambling.

> "*Derekh eretz kadma la-Torah.*"[5]
> "*Derekh eretz* (proper respect) takes precedence [even] over the study of *Torah*."

A discussion with my students on the meaning of this Rabbinic statement is the focus of the first session of Judaic studies courses which I teach. If we do not have the proper *derekh erekh* towards the material being studied, our fellow classmates and our teachers, we should not study *Torah*. Similarly, if we do not exhibit proper *derekh eretz* towards each other, our Jewish institutions and our teachers of *Torah*, we should not make believe that we are living a Jewish life.

Derekh eretz is the backbone of our existence as Jews. The essence of *Torah* is *derekh eretz*.

In the words of the *Jerusalem Talmud:*

> Rabbi Akiva stated, "…you shall love your neighbor as yourself…" (*Leviticus* 19:18); this is a great principle in the *Torah*.

Similarly, as reported in the *Talmud*, when asked to teach the entire *Torah* while standing on one foot, Rabbi Hillel stated:

> That which is despicable to you, do not do to your friend. This is the entire *Torah* and the rest is commentary, [now] go and study.
> (*Sabbath* 31a)

When we do not heed the words of Rabbi Akiva, Rabbi Hillel and our other Sages who teach us to treat each other with respect, we are doing what Latrell Sprewell did to his coach on December 1, 1997. We are attacking each other.

The *Torah* and the codes of Jewish law are replete with laws on how *derekh eretz* is properly implemented within a given society. Perhaps the greatest discussion on the Jewish legal treatment of this subject deals with the prohibition of speaking *lashon ha-ra* (true but negative statements), and other forms of prohibited speech.

In regard to *derekh eretz*, Jewish law is particularly sensitive to the treatment of parents, Rabbis and other teachers of *Torah*, the elderly and other potentially vulnerable people. In the Ten Commandments, God commands the Jewish people regarding the treatment of parents, "Honor your father and your mother" (*Exodus* 20:12).

We are bound by this commandment throughout our entire lives, even after our parents have passed away. We are commanded at all times to show them the ultimate in honor and respect.

The deference we must show our parents is so great that even if they publicly embarrass us, we are prohibited from doing anything to cause our parents any disrespect. One of the reasons why honoring parents is taken to such extremes is because along with our Rabbis and teachers, parents are responsible for providing us with a Jewish education, for teaching us *Torah*.

In a famous passage from Maimonides' *Mishneh Torah*, we are taught that in certain cases, the honor owed to one's Rabbi takes precedence even to the honor owed to one's own father!

In the words of Maimonides, quoting in part a passage from the *Talmud* (*Bava Metzia* 33a):

> Just as a person is commanded regarding the honor and fear of his father, so too is he obligated to honor and fear his Rabbi [and other teachers of *Torah*] even more than his own father. [This is so] since his father brings him into the life of this world and his Rabbi, who teaches him wisdom, brings him into the life of the world to come.
>
> (*Mishneh Torah, Hilkhot Talmud Torah* 5:1)

In the world of sports, the relationship between a parent and child or a Rabbi and student is most closely paralleled by the relationship between a coach and a player. Although a player may not always agree with his coach, he must always honor him.

P. J. Carlesimo has a reputation as a coach who can, at times, act in a provocative manner towards his players. In the words of *Newsweek*:

Carlesimo, a successful college coach at Seton Hall, has a profane, in-your-face style that has infuriated some of his pro players...[6]

Nevertheless, in spite of his sometimes unsavory disposition towards his players, Carlesimo is still the coach and by virtue of his office, he deserves the proper respect form his players — at all times.

Just as we are commanded to be especially respectful of our parents and our teachers of *Torah*, we are also commanded to be most respectful to the elderly and others who are potentially more vulnerable to abuse.

The *Torah* commands us:

Before someone who is old, you shall rise and you shall honor the presence of an elder....

(*Leviticus* 19:32)

We are also commanded to pay great respect to the elderly because of the great wisdom that they have acquired in their lifetime. In fact, our Sages teach that the Hebrew word for elder, *zaken*, is actually an acronym for *"zeh sh'kana hawkhma,"* or "he who has acquired wisdom."

The *Torah* specifically warns us to make sure that certain people who historically have been wronged are treated with proper respect. These individuals include the orphan and the widow. In the words of the *Torah*, "Every widow and orphan you shall not afflict" (*Exodus* 22:21).

Proper respect is a prerequisite for success in not only the Jewish world, but in every environment. Whether it be the home, workplace or the sports arena, we must exhibit appropriate honor and respect towards one another, in order for peace and harmony to exist. In sports this is known as (proper) sportsmanship. In Jewish tradition we refer to such behavior as *derekh eretz*. We are taught that we must honor our fathers, mothers and coaches!

We Don't Need Another Hero;
We Have Enough of Our Own!

In a national publication, a notice recently appeared seeking applicants to apply for the position of a hero or role model. Some job demands included that the applicant must "[be] perfect," citing that it is a 24 hour a day, 365 day a year job. The ad also stressed that there is a mandatory retirement as soon as a "scandal hits."

This fictitious ad, which appeared in an article by Rick Telander in a 1991 issue of *Sports Illustrated,* implies that we put impossible pressures on our heroes.[7] This is especially true of sports stars and other celebrities, who many times are not particularly well-suited role models for reasons other than the skills they exhibit in their professional lives.

One of the greatest athletes of all time, Michael Jordan, is an authority on this subject. "...People look to their role models to be almost flawless...," said Jordan. "It's hard to live up to something like that, really harder than basketball. It's really the biggest job I have."[8]

We have learned over the years that "to err is human" and that the nature of many human beings is to equate stardom on the playing field or on the silver screen with stardom in the world of moral virtues. Through the years, we repeatedly have been disappointed with fallen heroes such as "Shoeless Joe" Jackson, Steve Garvey, Michael Jackson, Magic Johnson and O. J. Simpson.

Why do we select athletes and other celebrity performers to be our heroes? After all, they haven't requested that we choose them!

One answer to this question is that it has been, and will probably always be, a human need to admire certain individuals and to learn from them in order to give us hope. Telander theorizes that it is only natural to choose sports stars as our heroes and our role models, since these people have achieved what people want most in life — certainty. After all, sports games have rules, boundaries, penalties and timeouts, which provide certainty. With certainty comes confidence, contentment and peace. Star athletes have demonstrated great success in mastering certainty.

In our lives we witness certainties as well. One certainty is that Americans have a need for heroes, while a second one is that we have a tendency to look towards sports stars and other celebrities as our heroes and our role models. How do we best balance the need for heroes and certainty?

We should view our sports stars as role models for only realistic qualities and not as "True Heroes." We should emulate them for such traits as dedication towards physical fitness, work ethic and sportsmanship. With rare exceptions, we should only emulate them for their on-field accomplishments. I refer to this modified type of hero as the "Limited Sports Hero."

Here are some of my Limited Sports Heroes:

- Michael Jordan, "MJ," remains a Limited Sports Hero strictly for his pure skill, his ability to entertain, his work ethic, and for his success in inspiring others to perform at higher levels.

- Pete Rose, in spite of his brush with the law and his banishment from Major League Baseball, is a *very* Limited Sports Hero for his outstanding on-field performance as a baseball player. He always ran to first base even when walked and as a baseball player, he exemplified the quality of "true Jewish competitiveness," living by the Rabbi Zusya Principle of working your hardest to achieve your potential.

- Hank Greenberg and Sandy Koufax are the only two Jewish Major League players to be inducted into the Baseball Hall of Fame. In addition to their outstanding performance, both Greenberg and Koufax identified as Jews and refused to play on *Yom Kippur* in spite of being desperately needed by their teams. Greenberg's refusal to play on *Yom Kippur* during a tight 1934 pennant race was the subject of a popular poem written by Edgar Guest. Both Sandy Koufax and Hank Greenberg are Limited Sports Heroes for doing that which is right and not succumbing to outside pressures.

- For similar reasons, Olympic swimming star Mark Spitz is another Limited Sports Hero. As an international celebrity in 1972, he openly identified as a Jew in the wake of the tragic Palestinian terrorist attack on Israeli athletes in Munich, Germany. Today, Mark Spitz volunteers with great pride for Maccabi USA/Sports for Israel. Spitz's identification as a Jew inspired many assimilated Jews to feel proud of their Jewish heritage.

- Among coaches and managers, my Limited Sports Hero is former Bulls coach Phil Jackson. From Jackson, I have learned such leadership virtues as the importance of always remaining calm in spite of the fast and sometimes frantic pace of life, and the importance of striving to win while balancing the diverse needs of a group.

- Among the owners of professional sports teams, one of my Limited Sports Heroes remains the late Bill Veeck, perhaps the most creative entrepreneur in the history of professional sports. To sports fans, Veeck, the former owner of the Cleveland Indians, St. Louis Browns and Chicago White Sox, exemplified a secular application of the Jewish principle of — *mi-tokh sh'lo li-sh'ma, ba li-sh'ma* — that a person who does the right thing, but for the wrong reason, eventually will do it for the right reason.

- Finally, Jerry Reinsdorf, Chairman of the Chicago White Sox and Bulls, is also a Limited Sports Hero. From Reinsdorf, I learn such important lessons as being straightforward with people and making tough decisions no matter how publicly unpopular they may be.

These happen to be some of my Limited Sports Heroes. Who should be our True Heroes? In the words of a song made famous by singer Tina Turner, "We don't need another hero!"[9] After all, we have enough of our own!

As Jews, we don't need to venture into the world of sports and entertainment to find our True Heroes; after all, we have plenty of our own. True Heroes are found in many different places. We simply must begin by studying Jewish history. Many great individuals who qualify as True Heroes are described in the *Torah, Prophets (Nevi-im), Talmud,* and in later historical writings. We have role models among our contemporary Rabbis and other Jewish community and world leaders. We find True Heroes among less known people such as our teachers, friends, parents, grandparents and other relatives. We should serve as the true role models and heroes for our children. All of our actions should be exemplary so that our children and grandchildren emulate and look to us as role models.

Here are some of my True Heroes:

- Perhaps my all-time favorite hero is Moses. The *Talmud* (*Nedarim* 38a) notes that Moses had many outstanding qualities. He was considered wise as well as strong. Above all, Moses was a humble, modest man:

  > And the man Moses was extremely humble, more so than any
  > other person on the face of the earth.
  >
  > (*Numbers* 12:3)

  Ironically Moses' most heroic traits resulted from his being blatantly flawed. We see a number of instances in the *Torah*, for example, where Moses exhibited such human shortcomings as taking on too much responsibility and being impatient. Moses also considered himself flawed since he had a speech impediment which he felt prevented him from becoming an effective leader. By overcoming this imperfection, Moses served as an inspiring example of how each of us can overcome any obstacle and "just do it!" Moses' imperfection and character helped make him a more effective leader because he was very tangible and approachable — he was very human.[10]

- Our Patriarch Abraham and Matriarch Sara are great role models for *gemilut ḥasadim*, the performance of acts of loving kindness. From their deeds, we learn about such important commandments and Jewish ideals as welcoming guests into our home (*hakhnasat orḥim*), visiting the sick (*bikkur ḥolim*), the presumption of innocence (*kaf z'khut*), and true faith and trust in God (*emunah* and *bitaḥon*).

- Maimonides, the revered Sephardic physician and Rabbi, serves as a role model for the importance of combining and applying secular and Jewish scholarship towards the betterment of the world and the human condition.

- From Rabbi Akiva and his wife, Rachel, who insisted that she would only marry the uneducated Akiva if first he committed himself to the study of Torah, we are taught the importance of studying *Torah* each day of our lives. I view Rabbi Akiva and the other nine Rabbis who we recall in the martyrology section of the *Yom Kippur* service as role models for making meaningful sacrifices during our lives, sacrifices which help ensure that our children and grandchildren study *Torah* and lead committed Jewish lifestyles.

• From Rabbi Akiva and Rabbi Hillel, I learn that the essence of *Torah* is performing the *mitzvah* of *ahavat Yisrael*; this means, in a homiletic sense, that we treat all people the way we ourselves wish to be treated.

• Among the leaders of the modern State of Israel, Menachem Begin remains my True Hero. As a young man living in Europe, he witnessed the Nazis shackle his beloved father and throw him into a river where he drowned. Menachem Begin learned from this and other acts of murder and anti-Semitism that in order for the Jewish people to survive, they must take care of themselves in a world where history has been consistently marred by hatred of Jews. Begin and his wife Aliza are to be admired for their convictions despite the feelings of the rest of the world. They remain role models of what Zionism is all about.

• Natan Sharansky is a role model for courage and standing up for one's beliefs. As a refusenik who was tortured and incarcerated by his Soviet captors, Sharansky refused to relent on his Zionist beliefs. Through the strength of his own convictions, along with the support of his loving wife Avital and countless others, in 1986, Natan finally realized his dream when he was set free, immediately immigrating to Israel.

• Three of the greatest Rabbinic leaders of the 20th Century are also my True Heroes. These distinguished leaders about all of whom we say *Zekher Tzaddik Li-v'rakha* (of blessed memory) are Rabbi Moshe Feinstein, Rabbi Joseph Baer Soloveitchik, and Rabbi Menachem Mendel Schneerson. These venerable Rabbis, who all have passed away within the last decade or so, brought the virtues of European Jewry to the United States. Rabbi Feinstein, one of the most highly regarded arbiters of Jewish law (*Poskim*) of all time, serves as a role model on how to apply Jewish law (*Halakha*) to daily contemporary life. Rabbi Soloveitchik, one of the all-time great Jewish philosophers, teaches us how to begin to reconcile Jewish philosophical issues. The *Lubavitch Rebbe*, Rabbi Menachem Schneerson, was one of the all-time leaders of inspiring Jews to become more observant and closer to tradition. The *Lubavitch Rebbe* serves as a role model to be accepting of all Jews and creatively spreading the message of Judaism (*Yiddishkite*) to others.

- In the "teenage world," we find a True Hero in the making in Maryland. Splitting time between the study halls of Pikesville's Talmudical Academy and the nearby basketball courts, one can observe Tamir Goodman. Goodman, a high school upperclassman, is known as "JJ," or the "Jewish Jordan" for his outstanding basketball skills. He is so talented that, as a high school junior, he received a scholarship beginning in the fall of 2000 to play basketball for the University of Maryland Terrapins. What is so unique about Tamir Goodman is that, in addition to being a star basketball player, he is an observant Jew. Maryland extended this scholarship to Goodman, knowing that Tamir will remain fully observant, which includes refusing to play basketball on the Sabbath. To me, Tamir Goodman qualifies as a "Teenage True Hero" for his ability to excel in the secular world, while remaining a committed Jew. After all, Tamir is a student of both *Torah* and secular studies, *shomer mitzvot* (observant) and an extraordinary athlete. I wish Tamir *hatzlaḥa* (success) in every way as he faces the unique challenges of an observant Jewish sports superstar.

- Aaron Mordecai Feuerstein, the CEO of Massachusetts-based Malden Mills, is another True Hero. In particular, he serves as a role model for the importance of practicing the principle of going over and beyond the letter of the law (*lifnim m'shurat ha-din*).

   One manifestation of this Jewish principle was demonstrated in the aftermath of a tragedy occurring on December 11, 1995. While celebrating his 70th birthday with family and friends that day, Feuerstein was informed that a serious fire had destroyed his factory. Undeterred and committed to the welfare of his employees, he immediately announced plans to rebuild the factory, and continued to pay salary and benefits to his employees. This act of kindness amounted to $1.5 million per week.

• Lou Weisbach, the Founder and President of HA•LO Industries, Inc., is another True Hero of mine. Weisbach serves as a role model for being a *ba-al tzedaka*, a philanthropist according to Jewish tradition. In addition to supporting numerous Jewish and civic causes, Lou reaches out to provide comfort, support and friendship to many people in need. Through his business acumen and creativity, he has made HA•LO the leader in the promotional products industry. The names of Lou Weisbach and HA•LO are familiar to sports fans across America as the HA•LO name is emblazoned on many Major League dugouts and at the United Center on chairs designated for the Bulls players. Lou Weisbach remains a True Hero, because he combines his love for business and sports with his even greater love of *ḥesed* (kindness) and *tzedaka*.

• Finally, my parents are and, God willing, will continue to be my True Heroes. Along with my grandparents, and my wife's parents and grandparents, all of blessed memory, I was taught both formally and by way of personal example. They have taught me the importance of believing in God at all times, despite the Holocaust and the other horrors of the world; respect and tolerance for humankind; the true meaning of Zionism; and the importance of combining and applying Jewish and secular education to help make our world a better place.

"We don't need another hero!" because we have enough of our own!

Let us all resolve to strive towards leading even more exemplary lives so that we can be True Heroes for our children and grandchildren for many, many more years to come.

- Glossary of Jewish Terms and Personalities
- Jewish Bibliography
- Notes

Introduction

The following **Glossary of Jewish Terms and Personalities** is a compilation of over 150 Jewish terms and personalities mentioned in this book. I hope the brief definitions provided are adequate to provide the reader with necessary information. Although phrases have been primarily used, where necessary, I have used full sentences. In providing accurate information throughout this book, I have referred to the books listed in the **Jewish Bibliography** which follows as well as other sources. The following books are all valuable resources for the Jewish home library and are, therefore, recommended.

GLOSSARY OF JEWISH TERMS

Aaron — The older brother of Moses who served as his spokesman, as well as the first High Priest (*Kohen Gadol*). Especially known for his love and pursuit of peace.

Abraham — The first of the three Patriarchs (*Avot*). Along with his wife Sara, he founded monotheism and the roots of the Jewish religion and people.

ahavat Yisrael — Literally, "love of Israel." Based upon *Leviticus* 19:18, this *mitzvah* directs all Jews to love each other. This was heavily promoted by both Rabbi Akiva and Rabbi Hillel.

Ahl ha-Nissim — The name of the special prayer recited on Ḥanukah in the *Amidah* and *Birkat ha-Mazon* prayers.

Akeidat Yitzḥak — The binding and near sacrifice of Isaac by Abraham.

Aleph-Bet — The Hebrew alphabet. The *alpeh* and *bet* are the first two letters of the alphabet.

aliyah — Literally, "ascension." The Hebrew/Yiddish term given to the honor of being called "up" to the *Torah* to recite the *Torah* blessings. *Aliyot* is the plural. On a weekday, the first *aliyah* is accorded to a *Kohen*, the second to a *Levi* and the third to a *Yisrael*. The term *aliyah* also refers to the act of immigrating to Israel.

Amidah — Literally, "(the) standing." A prayer recited while standing during all three daily prayer services. In weekday services this prayer is also referred to as the *Sh'moneh Esreh*. In *Halakhic* literature the *Amidah* is referred to as *Tefillah* (prayer).

anti-Semitism — The hatred of Jews which has existed since the days of Abraham.

Avodat Hashem — The service and worship of God.

Avot — The Hebrew term for the three Patriarchs: Abraham, Isaac and Jacob.

Baal ha-Turim — Rabbi *Yaakov Baal ha-Turim* (1275-1343 approx.) who authored the great *Halakhic* code known as the *Arba-ah Turim* (Four Rows). Also known as "The Tur."

Ba-Midbar — Known as *Numbers* in English, the Hebrew name of the fourth book of the *Torah*.

Bar Mitzvah — Literally, "son of commandment." Rite of passage for a Jewish boy when he turns 13 and one day, according to the Hebrew (lunar) calendar. At that age he becomes obligated to perform all commandments (*mitzvot*) incumbent upon Jewish men. *B'nei Mitzvah* is the plural.

Bartenura — *Rabbi Ovadiah Yarei of Bartenura* (1445-1500 approx.). A *Talmudist* who wrote a popular commentary on the *Mishnah*.

Bat Mitzvah — Literally, "daughter of commandment." Rite of passage for a Jewish girl when she turns 12 and one day, according to the Hebrew (lunar) calendar. At that age she becomes obligated to perform all commandments (*mitzvot*) incumbent upon Jewish women. *B'not Mitzvah* is the plural.

Begin, Menachem (1913-1992) — Great Zionist leader of Israel from pre-statehood until his death. This member of the *Likud* party served as Israel's Prime Minister from 1977-1983 and began the peace process by entering into the Camp David Accord.

Beit ha-Mikdash — The Hebrew term for the Holy Temples in Jerusalem. The first Temple was built by King Solomon and destroyed by the Babylonians in 586 B.C.E. The second Temple was built by Herod and destroyed by the Romans in 70 C.E. Today a part of the Western Wall, which surrounded the second Temple, remains.

Beit Hillel/Beit Shammai — The academies founded by two great Sages, Rabbi *Hillel* and Rabbi *Shammai*. The *mahaloket* (conflict or controversy) of *Hillel* and *Shammai* is used by our Sages in *Pirkei Avot* as an example of a type of *mahaloket* which is constructive and is "for the sake of Heaven" ("*l'shem shamayim*").

bikkur holim — The *mitzvah* of visiting the sick, which is in the category of *gemilut hasadim*, acts of loving kindness.

Birkat ha-Mazon — The Grace after Meals. This prayer is sometimes also referred to in Yiddish as "*bentchen*."

Birkat Kohanim — Literally, "priestly blessing." The three-fold blessing recited by the priests (*Kohanim*) when blessing the Israelites. Today this blessing is included in every *Amidah* which is repeated. This blessing is included as part of the *Birkat Banim* (parental blessing) and is first found in the *Torah* (*Numbers* 6:24-26).

bitaḥon — Trust or confidence (in God).

B'nei Yisrael — Literally, "the Children of Israel" (Jacob). It is sometimes also translated as the "Israelites."

bris — Literally, "convenant." The Yiddish/Hebrew (*Ashkenazic* dialect) for the ritual by which a Jewish boy is entered into the covenant of Abraham through circumcision on the eighth day of his life. In the Hebrew *Sephardic* dialect this is (fully) referred to as *"b'rit milah."*

Cain/Abel — The first two brothers in world history. The sons of Adam and Eve, these two men set a bad precedent for sibling rivalry.

Camp David Accord — Peace treaty entered into in 1978 between Israel and Egypt whereby Israel returned all the land it captured from Egypt in the 1967 Six Day War in exchange for Egypt's recognition of Israel's right to exist. Israel's Prime Minister Menachem Begin and Egyptian President Anwar Sadat received the Nobel Peace Prize for reaching this agreement which was facilitated by U.S. President Jimmy Carter.

daven — Yiddish for "pray."

derekh eretz — Literally, the "way of the land." This term usually refers to proper respect.

dina d'malkhuta dina — Literally, "the law of the kingdom is the law." *Halakhic* principle directing Jews, with few exceptions, to abide by the laws of the host country.

Devarim — Known as *Deuteronomy* in English, the Hebrew name of the fifth book of the *Torah*.

Ecclesiastes — *Kohelet*. Collection of philosophical insights authored by King Solomon (See: *Megillah*).

emunah — Faith or belief (in God). The word *"amen"* is derived from the same root.

Eretz Yisrael — The Land of Israel.

gabbai — In Talmudic times, the appointed official who collected and distributed community *tzedaka* funds. In contemporary times, the synagogue member who distributes *aliyot* and other honors and calls synagogue attendees up to the *Torah*. *Gabbaim* is the plural.

gemilut ḥasadim — Acts of loving kindness. A category of *mitzvot* which focus on helping others in need. They include *bikkur ḥolim* (visiting the sick) and *niḥum avel* (comforting the bereaved).

gimatriah — Hebrew numerology. A system by which Hebrew letters and words are given numerical values.

Golden Calf — The Israelites built this idol as a deity when Moses was on Mount Sinai to receive the *Torah*. In Hebrew, known as *Egel ha-Zahav*.

Greenberg, Hank — Hall of Fame slugging first baseman who played his career mainly with the Detroit Tigers. Along with Sandy Koufax, he is among the only two Jewish Major League players inducted into Baseball's Hall of Fame.

Haggadah — Literally, "(the) telling." The text used at the Passover *Seder* to retell the *Pesaḥ* story.

ḥai — Literally, "alive"/"lives." Since its *gimatriah* is 18, 18, along with multiples and fractions of 18, are considered "lucky" Jewish numbers (See: *gimatriah*).

hakarat ha-tov — Literally, "recognizing the good." A principle which directs the Jewish people to be optimistic and grateful.

Halakha — This term refers to the body of Jewish law whose ultimate primary sources are the *Torah* (Written Law) and the Oral Law transmitted at Sinai. Derived from the Hebrew verb *halakh* ("went" or "walked"), *Halakha* directs every Jew on how "to go," how to lead his/her life.

Halakhic — Pertaining to *Halakha*.

Hanna — Mother of the great prophet Samuel.

Ḥanukah — Literally, "dedication." The eight-day festival celebrating the miraculous Maccabean victory over the Assyrian-Greeks in 165 B.C.E. along with the miracle of the oil.

Hashem — Literally, "the name." An expression of God's name *Midat ha-Raḥamim*, as a compassionate God.

Ḥasidim — Usually refers to *Ḥasidic* Jews [i.e., those who follow a philosophy founded by Rabbi Israel *Ba-al Shem Tov* (1700-1760)]. *Lubavitch-Chabad* is one sect of *Ḥasidim*. In a colloquial sense, "*ḥasid*" refers to a follower of a certain Rabbi. The word "*ḥasid*" is related to the word "*ḥesed*," which means kindness or goodness.

havdala — Literally, "distinction" or "separation." The ceremony during which we bid farewell to the Sabbath, separating it from the rest of the week.

Ḥazal — The acronym for "*Ḥakhameinu Zikhronam Li-v'rakha*," "Our Sages of Blessed Memory."

Ḥazan — In *Talmudic* times the role of the *Ḥazan* included overseeing the activities of the Temple and synagogues. In contemporary Jewish communities, the term *Ḥazan* refers to a Cantor (i.e., a professional who leads the Congregation in the chanting of the prayer liturgy).

ḥesed — Kindness or goodness.

High Holy Days — Term used for *Rosh Hashanah* and *Yom Kippur*, a time when the Jewish people are especially focused on repentance (*teshuva*). In Hebrew, known as *Yamim Noraim*.

ḥol ha-moed — The non-*yom tov* days of *Pesaḥ* and *Succot*. Regarding ritual observance, these days are a hybrid of *yom tov* and secular days.

Holocaust — The destruction by the Nazis during World War II of over six million Jews, along with millions of others. In Hebrew known as *Shoah*.

ḥupah — The marriage canopy.

I.D.F. — Acronym for Israel Defense Forces (*Tz'vah Haganah L'Yisrael*).

Ishmael — The son born to Abraham and his concubine Hagar. The founder of the Arab people.

Jacob — The third of the three Patriarchs. This leader, lived a very difficult life marked by two long periods of separation from his father Isaac and then from his son Joseph.

Jewish day schools — Private schools in North America and other Diaspora countries in which, along with secular studies, a major part of the daily curriculum is devoted to religious studies.

Jewish Quality Time — Every Jewish parent, no matter how busy, must spend this with his/her children.

Joshua — Moses' successor as the leader of *B'nei Yisrael* (the Israelites). Along with

Caleb, Joshua was the only spy to make a positive report to the Israelites regarding the Land of Israel and their chances of conquering it.

Kabbalah — Jewish mysticism.

Kaddish — A prayer extolling God's holiness with several versions which can only be recited with a *minyan*. Colloquially, it usually refers to the Mourner's *Kaddish*.

kaf z'khut — Presumption of innocence.

kavana — Fervor or intention. This Hebrew term is derived from the same root as the word, *kivun*, "direction," and is most often used regarding prayer. When a Jew prays, it should be with great fervor and intention and should be directed to God.

kavod — The Hebrew or Yiddish term for "honor."

Ketuvim — The third main section of *Tanakh* (*Bible*). This section is comprised of 13 books, many of which were written during the period of the prophets. Included in *Ketuvim* are *The Five Megillot, Psalms* and *Proverbs. Ketuvim* is known in English by such names as *Scriptures, Writings* and *Hagiographa.*

kibud av v'em — The *mitzvah* (commandment) to honor our fathers and mothers. It is the fifth of the Ten Commandments (*Decalogue*).

Kiddush — The prayer recited over wine or grape juice to sanctify the Sabbath and all *Torah*-ordained holidays.

King Solomon — King of Israel (10th century B.C.E.). Son of King David, whose major accomplishments include the building of the first Temple and the authorship of *Ecclesiastes* and *Proverbs*. He was known in Hebrew as *Sh'lomo ha-Melekh.*

kippah — The Hebrew term for a man's skullcap. In Yiddish, it is known as a *yarmulkeh.*

K'lal Yisrael — Literally, "Israel Community." This term refers to the World Jewish Community.

Kohen — A man who is descended from Moses' brother Aaron, the first *Kohen Gadol* (*High Priest*). The plural is *Kohanim*. The *Kohanim* were in charge of the spiritual administration of the Temple.

Koraḥ — A cousin of Moses and Aaron who was so jealous of their leadership roles that he organized an (unsuccessful) rebellion against them.

korban — Hebrew word for sacrifice. It is derived from the same root as the word, *karov,* "close" or "near." The purpose of offering a sacrifice was to bring the donor closer to God. *Korbanot* is the plural.

kosher — Literally, "fit" or "proper." Refers to a status or procedure which is done in full compliance with Jewish law. This term is most commonly used to refer to food, *mezuzot* (parchments), a *Sefer Torah* (scroll) and *tefillin.*

Koufax, Sandy — Hall of Fame Dodgers pitcher who pitched four career no-hitters. Along with Hank Greenberg, he is among the only two Jewish Major League Baseball players inducted into Baseball's Hall of Fame.

kvetch — Yiddish for one who complains.

lashon ha-ra — Literally, "evil tongue." Truthful, but harmful speech, which is, with limited exceptions, prohibited by Jewish law.

layne — Yiddush for "read." Colloquially, refers to reading (chanting) from the *Torah.*

Leibowitz, Professor Nehama (1905-1997) — Bible scholar who devoted her lifetime to teaching *Torah* to Jews worldwide.

lifnim m'shurat ha-din — An *Halakhic* principle which guides every Jew to go over and beyond the letter of the law; to always try to capture the spirit of Jewish law without violating *Halakha.*

lulav and *etrog* — The four species blessed on *Succot.* The *lulav* is comprised of willow, myrtle and palm branches, while the *etrog* is a citron.

Maariv — The evening prayer service.

Maccabee — The extra name received by Judah and applied liberally to Judah's family, who led the Jewish charges against Antiokhus Epiphanes who attempted to force the Jews of Israel to abandon Judaism and assimilate into a Hellenistic society. Upon the successful overthrow of the Assyrian-Greek (*Yevanim*) government, the Maccabean family led the newly-formed Jewish government. Their government is referred to also as the Hasmonean dynasty.

Magen David — Literally, the "shield of David." This term also refers to the "star of David."

maḥaloket — Conflict or controversy.

Maimonides — Great Sephardic Rabbi and physician (1135-1204) whose works include the *Mishneh Torah* and *Moreh Nevukhim* (Guide to the Perplexed). Among his medical patients included the Sultan of Egypt. In Hebrew he was known as the *Rambam*.

Marah d'Atrah — Literally, "Master of the locale." This term describes, in part, the *Halakhic* authority of a Rabbi; any other person (Rabbi or lay) is prohibited from rendering *Halakha* or teaching in the domain of that Rabbi, without his express permission.

Mashiaḥ — The Hebrew term for Messiah, who, according to tradition, is descended from King David. One of the *Thirteen Principles of Faith* as promulgated by Maimonides is that a Jew must believe in the coming of the Messiah. When *Mashiaḥ* arrives, there will be peace and according to *Isaiah* 11:6, at that time "...a wolf will dwell with a lamb."

mazal tov — Literally, "good luck." This Hebrew/Yiddish greeting is also used as a congratulatory expression.

Megillah — Literally, "scroll." *Megillot* is the plural. In the *Bible*, refers to *The Five Scrolls* (*Ḥamesh Megillot*) of *Esther, Ruth* (*Rut*), *Ecclesiastes* (*Kohelet*), *Song of Songs* (*Shir ha-Shirim*) and *Lamentations* (*Eikha*).

Menorah — Candelabrum. This term usually refers to the *Menorah* in the Temple and *Mishkan* (Tabernacle). Although *Ḥanukiah* is a more precise term, it sometimes also refers to a *Ḥanukah* candelabrum.

mensch — Literally, "a man." A Yiddish term which refers to a good, decent, fair person.

menschlikhkite — What a *mensch* practices.

m'ḥila — Forgiveness.

midah — Ethical character trait. A man who exhibits good traits is referred to as a *ba-al midot*. In Yiddish or in the *Ashkenazic* dialect the plural of *midah* is pronounced as *midos*.

Midrash — The *Biblical* interpretations (*Halakhic* and legendary) of the *Tannaitic* Rabbinic Sages. Some of the *Midrashic* works include *Tanna D'vei Eliyahu Rabba, Sh'mot Rabba, Va-Yikra Rabba, Sifra* and *Tanḥuma*.

minyan — A group of ten or more Jewish men which is needed to recite certain prayers (*e.g.*, Mourner's *Kaddish*) at a religious service. *Minyanim* is the plural. Colloquially, it refers to a service at which a quorum is present.

Mi Sh'berakh — Literally, "(He) Who has blessed." A series of blessings said during the course of the *Torah* service. A special *Mi Sh'berakh* prayer is said for those who are ill.

Mishkan — The Tabernacle or Sanctuary built by the Israelites in the desert and used as the central place of worship before the Temple was built.

Mishnah — Literally, "study" or "teaching." This term usually refers to the *Halakhic* collection of *Tannaitic* texts edited by Rabbi Judah the Prince (died approx. 220 C.E.). Comprised of six sections known as *Sedarim* (Orders). Along with the *Gemarah*, this comprises the *Talmud*.

Mishneh Torah — Literally, "second *Torah*" or "repetition of the *Torah*." The *Halakhic magnus opus* of Maimonides completed in 1180. It is also referred to as *Yad ha-Ḥazakah* ("the strong arm"). *Hilkhot Matanot la-Evyonim*, a section in the *Mishneh Torah*, contains a comprehensive discourse on the laws of *tzedaka*.

mitzvah — Literally, "commandment." *Mitzvot* is the plural. Refers to a (*Torah-* or Rabbinically-ordained) religious commandment. Colloquially, it is used to mean a "good deed."

mitzvot bein adam la-ḥaveiro — Those commandments (*mitzvot*) between fellow Jews. They include *ahavat Yisrael* (loving our fellow Jew) and *kibud av v'em* (honoring our fathers and mothers).

mitzvot bein adam la-Makom — Those commandments (*mitzvot*) between a Jew and God. They include *Shabbat* (Sabbath) and *kashrut*.

mohel — The man who performs the *brit milah*. According to *Halakha*, it is the father's obligation to perform the *bris*. With few exceptions, the father is incapable of carrying out this awesome responsibility and, instead, discharges his obligation by appointing a *mohel*.

Moses — Born as a Hebrew, raised as an Egyptian prince and guided by God, he led the Israelites out of Egyptian slavery. A Hebrew prophet who was known as "*Moshe Rabbenu*" ("Moses Our Teacher").

Netanyahu, Yonatan (1946-1976) — On July 4, 1976, he led I.D.F. forces in the successful rescue of Jewish hostages held captive by terrorists in Uganda, during which he was killed. Yonatan's brother, Benjamin, was elected Israel's Prime Minister in 1996.

Nevi-im — The second main section of *Tanakh* (*Bible*). Comprised of 21 books, it tells the history of the Jewish people from immediately after the death of Moses to the time of the prophet *Malakhi*. Many of the books are named for the *navi* (prophet) whose prophecies and leadership are described in the given book. Some of the prophets for whom a book is named include Joshua, Isaiah, Ezekiel, Jonah and Micah.

nihum avel — The *mitzvah* of comforting the bereaved which is in the category of *gemilut hasadim*, acts of loving kindness.

parasha — Literally, "portion." Most often used to describe the weekly *Torah* portion (*parashat ha-shavuah*). Another term used is *sidra* (plural, *sidrot*). There are a total of 54, including *Noah, Bo, Yitro, Korah, Balak* and *Pinhas*.

parnasah — The means/ability to support oneself and one's family.

Passover — *Torah*-ordained holiday celebrating the exodus from Egypt of the Children of Israel. Celebrated for seven days in Israel and eight in the Diaspora. A highlight includes the *Seder*. In Hebrew this holiday is known as *Pesah*. In prayer liturgy Passover is sometimes referred to as "*z'man heiruteinu*," the "season of our freedom."

Pharaoh — The title of the King of Egypt during such periods of time as the years Joseph and the Israelites lived in Egypt.

Pirkei Avot — *Ethics of Our Fathers*. One of the few tractates in the *Talmud* with no *gemarah*. The theme of this tractate is the wisdom (*hawkhma*) of our Sages.

p'riya u-r'viya — The commandment to procreate. The first *mitzvah* commanded to men. A Jewish father fulfills this *mitzvah* once he has given life to a son and a daughter. *P'ru u-r'vu* is the Hebrew equivalent of this Aramaic term.

Purim — A festival celebrating the defeat of *Haman* and his anti-Semitic followers who attempted to kill the Jews of King Ahasuerus' kingdom.

pushkeh — Yiddish term referring to a container used to collect monies for charity (*tzedaka*). Sometimes also referred to as "pushkie."

qvell — A *Yiddish* term used to connote the experience and expression of great pride.

Rabbi — From the Hebrew *Rahbi*, "my master." Title conferred upon Jewish leaders upon their successful matriculation through a rigorous curriculum of Judaic studies. The focus of the curriculum of Orthodox-ordained Rabbinical students is to properly train these men to become *poskim* (arbiters of Jewish law). *Rebbe* is an endearing form of the title "Rabbi."

Rabbinate — The profession or calling of Rabbis.

Rambam — The Hebrew name of Maimonides. An acronym for *Rabbi Moshe Ben Maimon* (Rabbi Moses the son of Maimon) (See: *Maimonides*).

Rashi — Acronym for *Rabbi Shlomo Yitzhaki,* the French Rabbi (1040-1105 C.E.) who wrote the classic commentaries on the *Bible* and *Babylonian Talmud.*

refusenik — Term given to those Jews who applied to the former Soviet government for permission to emigrate from the U.S.S.R. and were "refused." Some of the better-known former-refuseniks include: Natan Sharansky, Yosef Begun and Ida Nudel.

Reinsdorf, Jerry — Chairman of the Chicago Bulls and Chicago White Sox.

Rosh Hashanah — Literally, "the head of the year." Refers to the Jewish new year celebrated at the beginning of the month of *Tishrei*. Begins the Ten Days of Penetence (Repentance).

Ruth — Heroine of *The Book of Ruth,* who converted to Judaism because of her love of the faith. Her conversion is used as a model for proper conversion. *The Book of Ruth* is read on *Shavuot*. King David is a descendent of Ruth.

Sara — The first Matriarch of Israel. The wife of Abraham and mother of Isaac is well remembered for both her outer and inner beauty.

Seder — Literally, "order." The special service conducted on Passover around the holiday (*Yom Tov*) table during which we retell the story of the exodus from Egypt. Highlights include the eating of bitter herbs (*maror*), vegetable (*karpas*), *haroset* and *matzah*, as well as the special focus in encouraging the participation of children.

Shabbat — The Jewish Sabbath, which begins at sunset on Friday and concludes at starset on Saturday night. It is a holy day especially devoted to prayer, *Torah* study and rest. In Yiddish and in the Hebrew *Ashkenazic* dialect, it is known as *Shabbos*.

Shaharit — The morning prayer service.

shalom — Hello, good-bye or peace. This Hebrew word is related to the word *shalem*, which means "whole" or "complete."

Shalom Bayit — Literally, "peace (of the) home." Refers to the sacred principle in Jewish tradition of maintaining tranquility in the home. Although *Sh'lom Bayit* is the grammatically correct form of this term, it is oftentimes referred to as *Shalom Bayit*.

shandeh — Literally, "shame" in Yiddish. Sometimes pronounced *"shanda."*

Shavuot — Known as the festival of "weeks," since it is observed seven weeks after the beginning of Passover. This holiday marks the anniversary of the giving of the *Torah*, along with the bringing of the first fruits (*bikurim*) to Jerusalem in the days of the Temple.

Shemini Atzeret — A special holiday ordained in the *Torah* which immediately follows *Succot*. Literally, "the eighth (day) of assembly."

shem tov — Literally, "a good name." Refers to a person's reputation.

sheva berakhot — Literally, "seven blessings." A series of (seven) blessings recited under the *hupah* (marriage canopy) and at special meals during the week following a couple's wedding.

shul — The Yiddish word for synagogue.

simha — The Hebrew and Yiddish word for a happy occasion. Many times, linked with the word *sasson* (joy).

Simhat Torah — Literally, "rejoicing of the *Torah*." A holiday, originated in the Middle Ages, on which we celebrate the conclusion and beginning of the reading of the annual cycle of *Torah* readings. This holiday is observed on *Shemini Atzeret* (in the Diaspora on the second day) and is celebrated with dancing and singing.

Simon Wiesenthal Center — Named after the famous Nazi hunter, this Los Angeles-based organization educates both Jews and non-Jews worldwide about the evils of hatred and bigotry, using the Holocaust as the most egregious example in world history.

sinat hinam — Literally, "free (unwarranted) hatred." The *Talmud* lists this as a main reason why the second Temple was destroyed.

Spitz, Mark — Former U.S. Olympic swimmer who won a total of nine gold medals including seven at the 1972 Munich games.

Steinsaltz, Rabbi Adin (born 1937) — A leading contemporary Rabbinic Scholar, Rabbi Steinsaltz continues to translate the *Talmud* (*Babylonian* and *Jerusalem*) into Hebrew. He has been likened to the *Rashi* of this generation, in that he is greatly contributing to the accessibility of the *Talmud* to the Jewish masses.

Strug, Kerri — A member of the U.S. women's gymnastics team which won the gold medal in women's gymnastics team competition in the 1996 Summer Olympic games in Atlanta.

Succot — Literally, "booths." A seven day festival which follows *Yom Kippur* and is highlighted by "dwelling" in specially-designed booths (*succahs*) and blessing the *etrog* and *lulav*.

synagogue — After the destruction of the Second Temple, this institution became the central place of Jewish worship. Led by Rabbis and supportive lay leaders, synagogues provide three main functions: house of worship (*beit tefillah*), house of study (*beit midrash*) and house of (social) gathering (*beit k'nesset*).

Szenes, Hannah (1921-1944) — Early Zionist leader and *Haganah* fighter who was killed while trying to save Allied prisoners of war held captive in Europe.

Talmud — The main work comprising the Oral Law. Comprised of the *Mishnah* and *Gemarah*. The *Jerusalem Talmud* was completed in approximately 390 C.E., whereas the *Babylonian Talmud* was completed in about 499 C.E.

Talmud Torah — Literally, "the study of *Torah*." The commandment to devote a part of each day to the study of the *Torah* or another traditional text. Arguably, the most important of the 613 *mitzvot*.

Tanakh — Acronym for *Torah, Nevi-im* (*Prophets*) and *Ketuvim* (*Scriptures*). The Hebrew term for *Bible*.

Taryag — Refers to "*Taryag Mitzvot,*" the 613 *Torah*-ordained commandments. The *gimatriah* of *Taryag* is 613 (See: *gimatriah*).

tefillin — Worn by men during the weekday (non-*Shabbat* or holiday) morning service. They are comprised of two black leather boxes each containing parchments on which passages from the *Torah* are written. These boxes are attached to the head and arm by leather straps. In English *tefillin* are known as "phylacteries."

Ten Martyrs — (*Asarah Harugei Malkhut*) — Ten great Rabbis who died while sanctifying God's name (*ahl kiddush Hashem*). The dedication of these ten Sages is especially remembered on *Yom Kippur* in a special section of the *Musaf* service.

Ten Spies — The leaders of ten of the tribes of Israel commissioned by Moses, who brought back a pessimistic report on the Children of Israel's chances of defeating their enemies and conquering the Land of Israel. A second report was brought back by Joshua and Caleb who reassured the Israelites that, with God's help, they would conquer the Land.

teshuva — Literally, "return." It is most commonly translated as "repentance." The special Sabbath between *Rosh Hashanah* and *Yom Kippur* is known as *Shabbat Shuva* (Return) or *Shabbat Teshuva*.

Tisha b'Av — The ninth day of the Hebrew month of *Av*. Many tragedies occurred in Jewish history on this day, including the destruction of both Temples. The day is devoted to fasting, the reading of *Lamentations* and other expressions of mourning.

Torah — *The Five Books of Moses*. In Latin, it is known as the *Pentateuch*. In Hebrew, it is also referred to as *Ḥumash*. The *Torah* is the basis of Jewish law (*Halakha*).

tzedaka — Literally, "justice." Refers to the system of charity as delineated in Jewish law. The leading authority on this subject is Maimonides.

tzedek — Justice or righteousness. *Tzedek* is a top Jewish priority, as stated in the Torah: *"Tzedek tzedek tirdof"* — "Justice, justice you shall pursue" (*Deuteronomy* 16:20).

Va-Yikra — The Hebrew name of the third book of the *Torah*. In English it is known as *Leviticus*.

yahrtzeit — Literally, "year's time." A Yiddish word referring to the anniversary of a person's death. Each year on this date, *Kaddish* is recited for the departed.

Yetzer ha-ra — The evil inclination. Along with the *yetzer ha-tov* (good inclination), the *yetzer ha-ra* is found in the heart of every human being.

Yiddish — Literally, "Jewish." The language spoken in Eastern European Jewish communities. A language with a Germanic base and a blend of Hebrew and other languages.

Yiddishkite — Yiddish for "Judaism."

Yisrael — Literally, "Israel." Refers also to an Israelite, a Jewish man who is neither a *Kohen* or *Levi*.

Yizkor — Literally, "May He (God) remember." The name of the special memorial service recited on *Yom Kippur, Shemini Atzeret*, Passover and *Shavuot*.

Yom Kippur — The Day of Atonement. Along with *Rosh Hashanah,* it comprises the High Holy Days. It is a day especially devoted to prayer, repentance and fasting.

Yom Tov — Literally, a "good day." Colloquially, the Hebrew/Yiddish term for a Jewish holiday. Maimonides limits this term to the sacred days of Passover, *Shavuot, Rosh Hashanah, Succot* and *Shemini Atzeret.*

Zionism — A movement which calls for the re-institution of an independent self-governing Jewish government in the Land of Israel. Different philosophies include Religious and Labor Zionism. Some of the early Zionists include Theodore Herzl, Ahad ha-Am, David Ben-Gurion, Menachem Begin and Rabbi Isaac Kook.

Zusya, Rabbi Meshulam (1700s) — A great *Hasidic Rebbe* who lived in Hanipoli. Especially known for telling inspiring stories.

JEWISH BIBLIOGRAPHY

The Biblical and Historical Background of Jewish Customs and Ceremonies. Rabbi Abraham P. Bloch. Ktav Publishing House, Inc., 1980.

Chapters of the Sages: A Psychological Commentary on Pirkey Avoth. Rabbi Dr. Reuven P. Bulka. Jason Aronson, Inc., 1993.

A Dictionary of the Targumim, the Talmud Babli and Yerushalmi, and the Midrashic Literature. Dr. Marcus Jastro. Title Publishing Company, 1943.

Encyclopedia Judaica. 17 vols. Keter Publishing House Jerusalem, Ltd., 1972.

Encyclopedia of Jewish Concepts. Philip Birnbaum. Sanhedrin Press, 1979.

The Book of Our Heritage. Rabbi Eliyahu Kitov. Feldheim Publishers, Ltd., 1978.

The Complete ArtScroll Siddur. Translation and Commentary by Rabbi Nosson Scherman. Mesorah Publications, Ltd., 1990.

The Complete Hebrew-English Dictionary. Reuben Alcalay. Massada Publishing Co., 1986.

Ellis Island to Ebbets Field: Sport and the American Jewish Experience. Peter Levine. Oxford University Press, 1992.

Encyclopedia of Jews in Sports. Bernard Postal, Jesse Silver and Roy Silver. Block Publishing Company, 1965.

Great Jews in Sports. Robert Slater. Jonathan David Publishers, Inc., 1983.

The Great Torah Commentators. Avraham Yaakov Finkel. Jason Aronson, Inc., 1996.

Jewish Literacy. Rabbi Joseph Telushkin. William Morrow and Company, Inc., 1991.

Jewish Sports Legends. Joseph Siegman. Brassey's Inc., 1997.

The Jewish Way in Death and Mourning. Rabbi Maurice Lamm. Jonathan David Publishers, Inc., 1981.

The Jewish Way in Love and Marriage. Rabbi Maurice Lamm. Jonathan David Publishers, Inc., 1980.

The Minhagim. Rabbi Abraham Chill. Sepher-Hermon Press, Inc., 1979.

The NCSY Bencher: A Book of Prayer and Song. David Olivestone (Editor and Translator). Olivestone, Inc./The Goldmark Group, 1997.

The Soncino Talmud. 18 vols. English edition, Soncino Press, 1938.

The Stone Edition ArtScroll Chumash. Edited by Rabbi Nosson Scherman. Mesorah Publications, Ltd., 1993.

The Stone Edition ArtScroll Tanach. Edited by Rabbi Nosson Scherman. Mesorah Publications, Ltd., 1996.

To Be a Jew: A Guide to Jewish Observance in Contemporary Life. Rabbi Hayim Halevy Donin. BasicBooks, 1991.

To Pray as a Jew: A Guide to the Prayer Book and the Synagogue Service. Rabbi Hayim Halevy Donin. BasicBooks, 1980.

NOTES

CHAPTER 1

Baseball: A Season for Being Born

1. In this book, the Hebrew has been transliterated in accordance with the *Sephardic* dialect. All consonants should be pronounced as they are in English with the exception of the *ḥ* (ח) and *kh* (ך,כ) which should be pronounced as the first letter in Hanukah.

2. I am grateful to my congregant, Mr. Marton Kander, for reminding me of this scene and its most powerful messages.

3. For further details regarding Jerry Garcia's abuse of drugs, please see: David Gates, "Requiem for the Dead," *Newsweek*, August 21, 1995, pp. 46+; "The Dead's 30-Year Acid Test," *Newsweek*, August 21, 1995, p. 52; and William F. Buckley, Jr., "Jerry Garcia, RIP," *National Review*, September 25, 1995, pp. 102+.

4. For further details regarding Mickey Mantle's abuse of alcohol, please see: Jill Lieber, "Time in a Bottle," *Sports Illustrated*, April 18, 1994, pp. 66+; Diane K. Shah, "The Legend of Number 7," *Newsweek*, June 19, 1995, p. 70; Richard Hoffer, "Mickey Mantle," *Sports Illustrated*, August 21, 1995, pp. 18+; Associated Press, "Farewell to a Baseball Hero," *Chicago Tribune*, August 16, 1995, Sports Section, pp. 1+; and Michael Precker, "Mantle's Widow Finally Steps Out of His Shadow," *Chicago Tribune*, October 27, 1996, Sports Section, pp. 5+.

5. Sometimes referred to as the Epicurean Statement, this is similar to certain Biblical phrases including *Ecclesiastes* 8:15 and *Isaiah* 22:13. For further details please see John Bartlett and Justin Kaplin (General Editor), *Bartlett's Familiar Quotations* (Boston: Little, Brown and Company, 1992), pp. 24 and 26.

6. Jill Lieber, "Time in a Bottle," *Sports Illustrated*, April 18, 1994, p. 74.

7. Associated Press, "Farewell to a Baseball Hero," *Chicago Tribune*, August 16, 1995, Sports Section, p. 1.

8. The *Torah* teaches in *Parashat Va-Ethanan* (*Deuteronomy* 4:15) "And you shall diligently preserve your souls..." (*"v'nishmartem m'od l'nafshoteikhem"*). This verse, in part, refers to the *mitzvah* of taking care of our health. We are not simply advised to take care of our health; we are commanded to do so! It is a *mitzvah*. Similarly, the *Torah* teaches in *Parashat Ekev* (*Deuteronomy* 8:3) "...not on bread alone does a person live, but rather, on everything which flows from the mouth of the Lord does a person live." (*"lo ahl ha-lehem l'vado yihyeh ha-adam..."*)

9. Rabbi Joseph Telushkin on pages 522-523 of his book *Jewish Literacy* (New York: William Morrow and Company, Inc., 1991), tells the following *Hasidic* story about a man who openly slandered the Rabbi of his community:

    > ...One day, feeling remorseful, he begged the [Rabbi] for forgiveness, and indicated that he was willing to undergo any penance to make amends. The [Rabbi] told him to take several feather pillows, cut them open, and scatter the feathers to the winds. The man did so, and returned to notify the [Rabbi] that he had fulfilled his request. He was then told, "Now go and gather all the feathers."
    >
    > The man protested. "But that's impossible."
    >
    > "Of course it is. And though you may sincerely regret the evil you have done and truly desire to correct it, it is as impossible to repair the damage done by your words as it will be to recover the feathers."

10. Cal Ripken, Jr., voluntarily removed himself from the line-up of the final home game of the 1998 season after the Orioles had been eliminated from the penant race. After this historic game, Ripken commented:

    > Baseball has always been a team game, and I've always thought the focus should be on the team, and there have been times during the streaks that the focus was on the streak, and I never felt totally comfortable with that. It just reached a point where I firmly believe it was time to change the subject and restore the focus back where it should be [Buster Olney, "Oriole Officials Yielded To Cal Ripken's Streak," *New York Times*, September 22, 1998, p. D11].

For further details regarding the end of Ripken's Iron Man Streak see: Buster Olney, "Proud and Stubborn And Oh So Classical," *New York Times,* September 21, 1998, pp. D1+; Buster Olney, "After 2,632 Games in a Row, Orioles' Ripken Sits One Out," *New York Times,* September 21, 1998, pp. A1+; and Tim Verducci, "Endgame," *Sports Illustrated,* September 28, 1998, pp. 10+.

11. Stated by Woody Allen in an interview, as documented in Bartlett and Kaplin, *Bartlett's Familiar Quotations,* p. 767.

12. Tim Verducci, "Endgame," *Sports Illustrated,* September 28, 1998, p.11.

13. "Was There Nothing Worth Fighting For?" a sermon presented by Rabbi Dr. Jacob J. Schacter, Rabbi of the Jewish Center in New York City and Founding Editor of *The Torah u-Madda Journal,* to the Chicago Board of Rabbis in 1996. Rabbi Schacter's sermon and story contributed to the inspiration that led me to write "2632, 613, Cal and Passion!"

14. At the end of the most powerful, passionate *U-n'taneh Tokef* prayer which we recite on *Rosh Hashanah* and *Yom Kippur,* we proclaim "(And) repentance, prayer and charity remove the evil decree" ("*u-teshuva u-tefilla u-tzedaka ma-avirin et roah ha-g'zeira*").

15. *Go Down Moses.* For a history of this song see Theodore Ralph, *The American Song Treasury* (New York: Dover Publications, Inc., 1964), pp. 177-178.

16. This quote is included in the guide for the exhibit *Stealing Home: How Jackie Robinson Changed America.* This exhibit appeared at the Simon Wiesenthal Center's *Beit Hashoah* Museum of Tolerance in Los Angeles, California from April 7 — June 30, 1997 (hereafter *Weisenthal Exhibit Guide*).

17. Jerome Holtzman, "Jackie Helped Nation, Not Merely Baseball," *Chicago Tribune,* April 16, 1997, Sports Section, p. 3.

18. *Wiesenthal Exhibit Guide.*

19. Ibid.

20. Stephan H. Norwood, Rabbi Abraham Cooper and Harold Brackman, "Teammates: Greenberg's Role in Jackie Robinson Story," *Chicago Jewish News,* August 15-21, 1997, p. 5.

21. The English translation of this *mishnah* is the verbatim translation of Rabbi Reuven Bulka as found in his edition of *Ethics of Our Fathers, Chapters of the Sages: A Psychological Commentary on Pirkey Avoth* (New Jersey: Jason Aronson, Inc., 1993). All translated excerpts of *Ethics of Our Fathers* found in my book are either identical to Rabbi Bulka's translation or are modified. Once again, I wish

to thank Rabbi Bulka for generously allowing me to use his translation of *Ethics of Our Fathers* in this manner.

22. Other examples of characters in *The Book of Ruth* with names pertinent to the bearer of the name include: *Naomi* — derived from the Hebrew word *naim* (pleasant); *Elimelekh* — meaning "my God is King," *Maḥlon* — derived from the Hebrew word *maḥala* (sickness); *Khilyon* — derived from the Hebrew word *kilayon* (destruction); and *Boaz* — meaning "in him there is strength."

23. Jonathan Fraser Light, on page 96 of his book *The Cultural Encyclopedia of Baseball* (North Carolina: McFarland & Company, Inc., 1997), attributes the actual origin of the "Black Sox" nickname to the following:

> During the 1918 season [White Sox owner Charles] Comiskey refused to pay for cleaning the team's uniforms and the players began wearing the increasingly dirty uniforms for weeks at a time. After a while they began to refer derisively to themselves as the Black Sox.

24. Eliot Asinof, *Eight Men Out* (New York: Henry Holt and Company, 1987), back cover.

25. Richard O'Brien and Hank Hersch (Editors), "The Hit King Compromise," *Sports Illustrated*, September 22, 1997, pp. 15+. For further details regarding Pete Rose's banishment, please see: Margaret Carlson, "Charlie Hustle's Final Play: An Unrepentant Pete Rose is Banned From His Beloved Game," *Time*, September 4, 1989, p. 64; Steve Wulf, "Score One for Integrity; Bart Giamatti Acted Forcefully in Banishing Pete Rose," *Sports Illustrated*, September 4, 1989, p. 172; and David Kindred, "A You-Bet-Your-Life Lesson," *The Sporting News*, August 28, 1995, p.6.

26. Recently basketball players from two universities, Arizona State and Northwestern University, were linked to illegal point shaving activities. At a later date, Northwestern football players were linked to illegal gambling activities associated with football games. Even though neither school was involved in these activities, these scandals, needless to say, have tarnished the good names of these institutions. For further details see: Peter Kendall and Douglas Holt, "Point-Shaving Pays Off in Shame and Suffering: Arizona State Basketball Scandal Reaches Out of Desert to Chicago," *Chicago Tribune*, December 14, 1997, Section 1, pp. 1 +; "A Point-Shaving Primer," *Chicago Tribune*, March 27, 1998, Sports Section, pp. 6+; Rick Morrissey, "Fixer, Point Shaver Tell All: Officials Hear Sad Stories of Pendergast, Lee," *Chicago Tribune*,

August 7, 1998, Sports Section, pp. 1+; Rick Morrissey, "Spin (Away) Control at NU: Barnett: Stain's on the Individuals," *Chicago Tribune*, December 4, 1998, Sports Section, pp. 1+; Matt O'Connor, "U.S. Indicts 4 NU Players on '94 Team: Perjury Alleged in Football Betting," *Chicago Tribune*, December 4, 1998, Section 1, pp. 1+; and Bill Dedman, "Gambling Becomes the Talk of a Campus," *New York Times*, December 6, 1998, Section 1, p. 25.

27. For further details regarding the controversial remarks made by Campanis, Snyder and Zoeller and their aftermath see: Jonathan Rowe, "The Greek Chorus, Jimmy The Greek Got It Wrong But So Did His Critics," *Washington Monthly*, April 1988, pp. 31+; John Feinstein, "Tiger's Tempest in a Teapot," *Golf Magazine*, July 1997, pp. 20+; "The Odds on Jimmy," *The New Republic*, February 8, 1988, pp. 8+; and "Jimmy The Greek: Bizarre Excursion Into Racial History Costs Him His Job At CBS," *People Weekly*, February 1, 1988, p. 35.

28. Tom Verducci, "The Greatest Season Ever," *Sports Illustrated*, October 5, 1998, pp. 38-39.

29. Pauline Dubkin Yearwood, "A Magical Season," *Chicago Jewish News*, October 2-8, 1998, p. 18.

30. Gary Smith, "The Race Is On," *Sports Illustrated*, September 21, 1998, p. 50.

31. Michael Bamberger, "Sammy Sosa Showed He's Indeed The Man — Even When He and The Cubs Are Struggling," *Sports Illustrated*, September 28, 1998, p. 47.

32. For further information regarding the special relationship that Mark McGwire shares with his son, see Rick Reilly, "The Good Father," *Sports Illustrated*, September 7, 1998, pp. 32+.

33. See "Pray Ball! Take Me Out to the *Minyan*" in this book.

34. Rabbi Telushkin, "*Hasidim* And *Mitnagdim*: Israel *Ba'al Shem Tov* (1700-1760)," *Jewish Literacy*, p. 216.

CHAPTER 2

Basketball: A Season for Dancing

1. Richard Corliss, "False Hoops," *Time*, October 24, 1994, p. 76.

2. Dr. Martin Luther King, Jr., "I Have a Dream" (delivered at the Civil Rights March on Washington, D.C. on August 28, 1963), *The Annals of America*

1961-1968: The Burdens of World Power (vol. 18) (Chicago: Encyclopaedia Britannica, Inc., 1976), s.v. "Martin Luther King, Jr.: I Have a Dream," pp. 156-159.

3. Nehama Leibowitz, *Studies in Bereshit (Genesis)* (Jerusalem: Jewish Agency, 1976), p. 298.

4. Written in celebration of the six NBA Championships of the Chicago Bulls (1990-1991; 1991-1992; 1992-1993; 1995-1996; 1996-1997; 1997-1998).

5. See *Rashi*'s commentary to *Numbers* 8:2, "*ya-i-ru shivat ha-nerot*" and *Numbers* 8:4, "*miksha.*"

6. See *S'forno's* commentary to *Numbers* 8:2.

7. Written in celebration of the fifth NBA Championship of the Chicago Bulls (1996-1997). Similarly, in celebration of the Bulls third and fourth championships, I wrote messages regarding the significance of the numbers three and four in Jewish tradition. Since all three of these messages are rather technical, I have chosen to include only a simplified version of "Who Knows Five?"

8. Written in celebration of the sixth NBA Championship of the Chicago Bulls (1997-1998).

9. Rabbi Hayim Halevy Donin, *To Be a Jew: a Guide to Jewish Observance in Contemporary Life* (U.S.A.: BasicBooks, 1991), p. 121.

10. Ira Berkow, "The Jordan Decision May Be His Coach's," *New York Times*, June 8, 1998, p. C6.

11. When the strike-shortened 1998-1999 NBA season began, the composition of the Chicago Bulls was much different than it was during the previous season. Some changes included the retirement of Michael Jordan; the departure of Coach Phil Jackson; Tim Floyd's appointment as the Bulls new coach; the trading of Scottie Pippen to the Houston Rockets; and Dennis Rodman's departure.

12. For a discussion regarding my definitions of "True Hero" and "Limited Sports Hero" see "We Don't Need Another Hero; We Have Enough of Our Own!" in this book.

13. Bruce Handey and Jamie Malanowski, "It's All About Timing: That's Why, Nine Seasons into One of TV's Greatest Runs, Jerry Seinfield Called It Quits," *Time*, January 12, 1998, pp. 78-79.

14. Bonnie DeSimone, "Michael Jordan Retires: 'Exactly the Way I Wanted to End

It' — He Turns His Focus to Raising Kids," *Chicago Tribune*, January 14, 1999, Section 1, p. 22.

15. For an in-depth discussion regarding this interpretation see Rabbi N. Scherman (Editor), *The Stone Edition ArtScroll Chumash* (Brooklyn: Mesorah Publications, Ltd., 1993), pp. 544-545.

16. For further details regarding this matter, see: Rick Reilly, "Patriot Games," *Sports Illustrated*, March 25, 1996, pp. 53+; Frank Deford, "Of Stars and Stripes," *Newsweek*, March 25, 1996, p. 64; Curtis Bunn, "Players' Union Supports Abdul-Rauf," *Knight-Ridder/Tribune News Service*, March 14, 1996, p314K4652; Andrew Bagnato, "NBA Action Raises Anthem Ante: Suspended Player Took Stand on Faith," *Chicago Tribune*, March 14, 1996, Section 1, pp. 1+; and Sam Smith, "Abdul-Rauf Changes Stance: Plans to Rise and Pray While Anthem Plays," *Chicago Tribune*, March 15, 1996, Sports Section, pp. 1+.

17. Frank Deford, "Of Stars and Stripes," *Newsweek*, March 25, 1996, p. 64.

18. Curtis Bunn, "Players' Union Supports Abdul-Rauf," *Knight-Ridder/Tribune News Service*, March 14, 1996, p314K4652.

19. Although Dennis Rodman manifests, at times, exemplary off-court behavior, this is far less visible than and greatly overshadowed by his non-exemplary behavior. Deep down, I like Dennis Rodman; I only wish that he would seek the appropriate assistance to prevent himself from self-destruction and use his celebrity status to be a positive example for our youth!

20. For further information regarding this unfortunate incident and its aftermath see: Terry Armour, "Rodman: 'Here We Go': Kick Injures Courtside Cameraman," *Chicago Tribune*, January 16, 1997, Sports Section, pp. 1+; Terry Armour, "One Fine Day on the Way: Suspension Also Likely for Rodman," *Chicago Tribune*, January 17, 1997, Sports Section, pp.1+; Sam Smith, "A Foot for a Foot: NBA Must Kick Out Rodman for Season," *Chicago Tribune*, January 21, 1997, Sports Section, p. 6; Terry Armour, "Be Good...Or Else: NBA Reinstates Rodman, But Next Gaffe Will Be Last," *Chicago Tribune*, February 5, 1997, *Sports Section*, pp. 1+; and Sam Smith, "Stern Was Wrong to Back Off," *Chicago Tribune*, February 5, 1997, Sports Section, pp. 1+.

21. Terry Armour, "Be Good...Or Else: NBA Reinstates Rodman, But Next Gaffe Will Be Last," *Chicago Tribune*, February 5, 1997, Sports Section, p. 4

22. Ibid., p. 1.

CHAPTER 3

Football: A Season for Wrecking and Building

1. For further details please see Eliyahu Kitov (Translation by Nathan Bulman), *The Book of Our Heritage (Sefer Ha-Toda'ah)* (Jerusalem/New York: Feldheim Publishers, Ltd., 1978), p. 286.

2. *Antiokhus* tried to force his Jewish subjects to adopt Hellenism. Ironically, a part of this philosophy was an overemphasis of the importance of the human body and its physical beauty. In promoting this, *Antiokhus* "over-encouraged" participation in sporting activities. The method of forcing others to adopt Hellenism, is an example of using sports in a most negative manner!

3. Rabbi Ben-Tzion Firer, *Eleh Hem Moadai* (Tel Aviv: Rubinstein's Printing, n.d.), Part 3, pp. 17-19.

4. Along these lines, CNN's Larry King writes in the introduction of his book *Powerful Prayers* (Los Angeles: Renaissance Books, 1998), Larry King (with Rabbi Irwin Katsof):

    > ...I knew absolutely nothing about prayer. Well, almost nothing.

    > I prayed during the 1949 World Series when the Brooklyn Dodgers faced their uptown rivals, the New York Yankees. That year, every Dodgers fan prayed for victory but we all discovered, much to our disappointment, that God was a Yankees fan — the Dodgers lost four games to one. The Yankees outplayed us and the Yankees fans outprayed us...

5. In January 1999, Gary Barnett left Northwestern to become the head coach of the University of Colorado football team.

6. College athletics and its "powers that be" have continued to represent their top priority as promoting the academic best interests of the student-athlete and, in turn, the academic integrity of the university. Unfortunately, among too many universities, this ideal does not represent reality. Northwestern, on the other hand, has been one of the relatively few Division I schools which has refused to relax its tough academic standards, even for star athletes.

CHAPTER 4

Hockey: A Season for Crying and Laughing

1. This concept is developed further by the classical commentators in their analysis of *mitzvat ma-akeh,* the commandment to build a fence around a functional roof (See: *Deuteronomy* 22:8).

2. Bill Menezes, "Two Athletes Fight Their Way Back to Greatness," *Boys Life,* December 1993, p. 32.

3. Steve Marantz, "Time Is Throwing a Curve to Heroic Jim Abbott," *The Sporting News,* March 31, 1997, p. S24.

CHAPTER 5

Golf: A Season for Scattering and Gathering Stones

1. Harry Chapin and Sandy Chapin, "Cat's in the Cradle," 1974.

2. Alex Tresniowski, Tom Cunneff, Lynda Wright, Don Sider, and Joanne Fowler, "Rising Son," *People Weekly,* June 16, 1997, p. 99.

3. Earl Woods with Peter McDaniel, *Training a Tiger: A Father's Guide to Raising a Winner in Both Golf and Life* (New York: HarperCollins Publishers Inc., 1997), p. 7.

4. Sue Shellenberger, "Executives Reflect on Choices Made for Family and Career," *Wall Street Journal: Career News,* December 31, 1997: 3 pages. Online. Internet. Available http://www.wsj.com/public/current/articles/ SB868659511472569000.htm. The quote, or a variation of it, has been used by various individuals, including Rabbi Harold Kushner in his book *When All You've Ever Wanted Isn't Enough* (New York: Summit Books, 1986) at page 161.

CHAPTER 6

Sports Agency: A Season for Silence and Speaking

1. On page 149 of Dick Allen and Tim Whitaker's book, *Crash: The Life and Times of Dick Allen* (New York: Ticknor & Fields, 1989), Dick Allen gives the following explanation regarding his brotherly involvement:

> "...I wanted Hank to get that pension. He's my brother. I mentioned to the Sox how close he was to getting those days

under his belt. Chuck [Tanner, the Sox manager] said, 'Let's bring Hank home with that pension, Dick.' That was it. Hank didn't have the same skills I had on the baseball field. But he had the same desire. He was a good guy to have on a team. His desire to win would infect the rest of the guys on the pine."

2. See Frank Lidz, "Whatever Happened to... Dick Allen," *Sports Illustrated*, July 19, 1993, p. 84.

3. Eric Zorn, "Dumping Zorich, Pride of Chicago, Is Shame of Bears," *Chicago Tribune*, October 30, 1997, Section 2, p. 1.

4. Darryl Howerton, "Show Leigh the Money," *Sport*, September 1997, p. 71.

5. I am grateful to my congregant Mr. Ron Kritzman for sharing this "story" with me.

6. Dean David T. Link, "Law Schools Must Lead Legal Profession Back to Its Roots," *Chicago Tribune*, September 1, 1995, Section 1, p. 27.

7. Additional programs provided by The Decalogue Project include its Voluntary Mediation Program, Speakers Bureau and its annual community educational forum. For a more in-depth analysis of this author's views on the importance of contract representation for Jewish community professionals, please see Rabbi James M. Gordon, J.D., "Representing the Rabbi and Other Jewish Community Professionals in Contract Negotiations: A Model Program" (Chicago: The Decalogue Society of Lawyers, 1997).

CHAPTER 7

The Olympics: A Season for Peace

1. On January 6, 1994, Nancy Kerrigan was physically attacked after a skating practice in Detroit. Police reportedly suspected that the main objective of the attack was to enhance Tonya Harding's chances of beating Nancy Kerrigan in amateur skating competition. In connection to the Kerrigan assault, on March 16, 1994, Harding pled guilty to committing the Class C felony of "hindering prosecution." For further details see: E.M. Swift, "A Done Deal," *Sports Illustrated*, March 28, 1994, pp. 32+; Bernie Lincicome, "Pain, Grief Over (And So Is Skating)," *Chicago Tribune*, February 26, 1994, Sports Section, pp.1+; and John Rolfe, "The Attack on Nancy Kerrigan," *Sports Illustrated for Kids*, March 1994, p. 12.

2. E.M. Swift, "Give Young Athletes a Fair Shake," *Sports Illustrated*, May 2, 1994, p. 76.

3. For further details regarding the "McGwire-Sosa competition," please see "*Sasson v'Simḥa* (Joy & Happiness): Of Home Runs & *Succot*," in this book.

CHAPTER 8
Leaders and Heroes: A Season for Loving and Hating

1. Alexander Wolff, "Dean Emeritus," *Sports Illustrated*, October 20, 1997, pp.64-65.

2. This quotation is from Jerry Kramer, *Instant Replay* (New York: Signet Books, 1969) and is included in David L. Porter (Editor), *Biographical Dictionary of American Sports: Football* (Connecticut: Greenwood Press, Inc., 1987), s.v. "Lombardi, Vincent Thomas 'Vince'," pp.352-355.

3. When the strike-shortened 1998-1999 NBA season began, Latrell Sprewell was a member of the New York Knicks.

4. For further details regarding this unfortunate incident, please see: Mike Wise, "N.B.A. Star Who Choked Coach Wins Reinstatement of Contract," *New York Times*, March 5, 1998, pp. A1+; Selena Roberts, "The Reaction: Support Below but Dismay on High," *New York Times*, March 5, 1998, p. C1; Ira Berkow, "Choke Your Boss? Play In the N.B.A.," *New York Times*, March 5, 1998, p. C22; and Phil Taylor, "Center of the Storm," *Sports Illustrated*, December 15, 1997, pp. 60+.

5. A Rabbinic statement apparently derived from *Tanna D'vei Eliyahu Rabba* and *Va-Yikra Rabba.*

6. Mark Starr and Allison Samuels, "Hoop Nightmare," *Newsweek*, December 15, 1997, p. 28. See also Phil Taylor, "Center of the Storm," *Sports Illustrated*, December 15, 1997, pp. 60+.

7. Rick Telander, "The Wrong People for the Job," *Sports Illustrated*, December 23, 1991, p.108.

8. Ibid.

9. Graham Lyle and Terry Britten (Composers of Words and Music), "We Don't Need Another Hero (Thunderdome)," 1985.

10. Moses overcame the handicap of a speech impediment through God's appointment of his brother Aaron to serve as Moses' spokesman (see *Exodus*

4:10-17). This is similar to the recent legal victory won by pro golfer Casey Martin. A circulatory disorder in his leg restricts Martin from walking a golf course during tournament play. When the PGA prohibited Martin from using a golf cart during competition, Martin sued the PGA under the Americans With Disabilities Act. A U.S. Magistrate ruled that Martin could ride in a cart during the PGA tournaments. Just as the Almighty ruled that the support of a brother is a "reasonable accomodation" for a handicapped leader, the use of a golf cart is a "reasonable accomodation" for a handicapped golfer.